T0208660

Touched With Instructions

EYANA ADAH MCMILLAN

WESTBOW
PRESS
A DIVISION OF THOMAS NELSON

WestBow Press books may be ordered through booksellers or by contacting:

WestBow Press
A Division of Thomas Nelson
1663 Liberty Drive
Bloomington, IN 47403
www.westbowpress.com
1-(866) 928-1240

ISBN: 978-1-4497-0989-1 (sc)
ISBN: 978-1-4497-0990-7 (hc)
ISBN: 978-1-4497-0985-3 (e)

Library of Congress Control Number: 2010941850

Printed in the United States of America

WestBow Press rev. date: 05/26/2011

Praise, Dedication, and Thank You

To God be the glory for calling me to write this book. May He be praised for all He has done to release this book so we may continue to learn and grow in Him. Thank you, Lord, for Your love, encouragement, instruction, correction, and guidance in leading me through this work.

I dedicate this book to my parents, Elder Leighton E. and Evangelist Dr. Deborah M. McMillan. Thank you for loving and raising me and for making sacrifices for my benefit. You are truly examples of how we are to live holy, committed, and obedient lives that please the Lord.

I say a special thank you to my brothers, Nate Pritchard, Leighton McMillan Jr., Brandon McMillan, and Jonathan McMillan, for encouraging and challenging me and for making me laugh. You are truly my brothers in the Lord. Brandon, God bless you for the artwork you did for the book cover.

I also thank my pastor, Elder Charles S. Johnson Jr., and his wife—and my spiritual mentor—Evangelist Geraldine Jeanette Johnson, for the prayers, support, and confirmations you ministered to me as the Lord led you. Thank you, fellow members of Tabernacle Deliverance Church of God in Christ, for all your prayers and support.

Thank you, Evangelist Adrienne Banks, for allowing the Lord to use you to mentor me through the challenging times of writing. You are indeed precious and powerful in the Lord, and I admire the passion you have for Him. I also thank Sister Connie Beattie, who told me years ago that the Lord would use me to write books for Him.

I honor the memories of my grandparents, Deacon Horace and Mother Emma McMillan, and the Reverend Irvin and Minister Margaret Kittrell. They showed me how to love the Lord and instructed me to let the Lord have His way in my life.

Thank you, readers, for making the investment and taking the time to receive instructions the Lord has presented in this book. May the Lord deeply touch your lives and enrich you with His wisdom.

> *The fear of the Lord is the instruction of wisdom; and before honour is humility* (Prov. 15:33).

About the Cover Art

The artwork's title is "Touched."

Brandon K. McMillan, brother of the author, did this work.

It depicts an angel instructing the apostle Peter on how to escape prison and a ruler's execution plan.

> *Peter therefore was kept in prison: but prayer was made without ceasing of the church unto God for him. And when Herod would have brought him forth, the same night Peter was sleeping between two soldiers, bound with two chains: and the keepers before the door kept the prison. And, behold, the angel of the Lord came upon him, and a light shined in the prison: and he smote Peter on the side, and raised him up, saying, "Arise up quickly." And his chains fell off from his hands. And the angel said unto him, "Gird thyself, and bind on thy sandals." And so he did. And he saith unto him, "Cast thy garment about thee, and follow me" (Acts 12:5-8).*

Contents

Introduction
Touched With Instructions

Don't waste God's touch.

His touches are more than emotional experiences that cause us to shed a few tears or make us feel some type of wonderful peacefulness we never had before.

With His touches come creation, healing, freedom—and instruction.

We can deepen our relationship with the Lord by going beyond just knowing that He touched us. The Lord encourages us to seek Him to understand why He touches us and what to do with His touches.

Throughout the Bible, we see that exchanges of touch between Heaven and humankind came with instructions.

The Book of Genesis shows us how God created the heavens and the earth. He then touched the ground to form a man named Adam and instructed him to have dominion over the earth.

Genesis 32 details the wrestling experience Jacob had with an angel of the Lord. At the end of this all-night bout, the angel "touched the hollow of his thigh; and the hollow of Jacob's thigh was out of joint" (Gen. 32:25). The angel told the wrestling Jacob to let go, but Jacob wanted to be blessed first.

Before Jacob received any blessing, he received instruction about his identity. In past years, Jacob had done some underhanded things against his family members, including conning his blind father into believing that he (Jacob) was Esau, his twin brother. By doing so, Jacob deceitfully obtained Esau's inheritance.

The angel informed him that he was no longer Jacob—meaning trickster, con artist, or supplanter—but "Israel," a prince who has "power with God and with man, and hast prevailed" (Gen. 32:28).

Daniel 9 also notes the connection between touch and instruction. Daniel was praying for Israel, confessing the nation's sins while seeking God's forgiveness and help.

"Yea, whiles I was speaking in prayer, even the man Gabriel, whom I had seen in the vision at the beginning, being caused to fly swiftly, touched me about the time of the evening oblation. And he informed me, and talked with me and said, 'O Daniel, I am now come forth to give thee skill and understanding'" (Dan. 9:21–22).

The angel Gabriel goes on to instruct Daniel on God's plans for the nation.

The Lord so values the touch-instruction connection that He responds when we reach out to Him in faith.

Consider the powerful example found in Mark 5:24–34.

Jesus was in Capernaum, thronged by a crowd of people. Among them was a woman who suffered from a devastating illness for twelve years. She crawled through the people, desperate to reach Jesus. She stretched out her hand.

For she said, "If I may but touch his clothes, I shall be whole" (Mark 5:28).

When she touched the garment, Jesus felt virtue, or power, go out of him. In verse 30, He turned around and asked, "Who touched my clothes?"

When the woman revealed herself and her situation, Jesus addressed the woman, repeating back to her the "be whole" instructions that came with her touch.

And he said unto her, "Daughter, thy faith hath made thee whole; go in peace and be whole of thy plague" (Mark 5:34).

Mark 1:40–42 shows us how a man with leprosy experienced the compassionate touch of Christ, who disregarded societal rules to have no contact with people suffering from the often-contagious disease:

And there came a leper to him, beseeching him, and kneeling down to him, and saying unto him, "If thou wilt, thou canst make me clean." And Jesus, moved with compassion, put forth his hand, and touched him, and saith unto him, "I will; be thou clean." And as soon as he had spoken, immediately the leprosy departed from him and he was cleansed.

We will revisit these healing experiences as we continue learning about being touched with instructions. At that time, we will discover several nuggets of wisdom in the leprous man's interaction with Jesus.

We also will learn the blessings of touching Jesus while developing an intimate relationship with Him. By examining several biblical examples, we'll grasp how powerful touch and instruction can be, as function is revealed to creation, identities are changed, skills and understanding are imparted, wholeness and peace are granted, and the ostracized are cleansed and restored.

As the Lord leads us through this book, we will have moments of prayer, praise, repentance, and rededication.

We are now ready to continue our "Touched With Instructions" teaching by studying Apostle Peter's miraculous rescue detailed in Acts 12:1–11. We will see how God used connection and direction to deliver this apostle from prison and a death sentence.

Remember, God does not waste touches. Neither should we.

CHAPTER 1

Touched to Get Out

Peter was just hours away from an execution planned by King Herod, who thought that killing the apostle would stop the church's momentum. Herod had beheaded James, the first of Jesus' twelve disciples to be martyred. Acts 12:5 shows the church was praying without ceasing for Peter. God's answer was to send an angel equipped with instructions designed to rescue the apostle. Thus, Peter would have to obey the Lord's way out of captivity and out of Herod's death sentence.

When we are stuck in difficult situations, we can ask pastors, prayer partners, and loved ones to keep us in prayer. However, we must follow Peter's example of adhering to God's instructions concerning our circumstances. The church can pray for us, but not obey for us.

In Acts 12:6, we see that Peter is sleeping in prison. Suddenly, an angel appears and a bright light shines in the cell. The angel strikes the sleeping apostle on the side, ordering him to prepare for escape (verse 7). Peter's miraculous exit begins as shackles fall from his hands and feet.

This is the part where we get excited about Peter's experience and about our own touching encounters with the Lord.

"Jesus touched me."

"I saw the light!"

"The chains just fell off me, and I felt the burdens being lifted. I feel so free."

That's great.

However, consider this: Peter received a touch from the kingdom, but he was still in prison. His execution schedule was still in effect. Thus, it is possible to be touched and not be free.

There are people who go to church, get touched, and feel good. However, they are still in captivity to habits. They are rude at restaurants and impatient in food store lines. They engage in road rage while driving cars displaying "Jesus loves you" bumper stickers.

Are we the ones who felt the chains fall off but are yet wounding and shackling people exposed to our character flaws?

Let us be honest. Some of us claim the Lord has touched us. However, we are still proud, selfish, disobedient, and unfaithful in Bible study and prayer. We still generate excuses for ungodly behaviors, saying, "Please be patient with me; God is not through with me yet."

By the way we're behaving, it doesn't seem like God got started.

Many of us are having incredible church experiences. We're having a good time clapping, waving our hands, celebrating great preaching, crying out to God, and worshipping with other believers. However, we don't realize we're having church in jail.

Satan—who operated through Herod in attempts to stop the works of Peter and the early church—is still determined to destroy God's people today. He does not mind that people have moments of spiritual bliss, as long as they are in the place he put them when he arrives to destroy them.

Remember, Satan was once Lucifer, an angel of light who experienced the magnificence of heaven and the glory of God's presence. Wanting the heavenly throne, he fought against God and lost. Furthermore, Satan has seen God's miracles on the earth. Demons believe in God and tremble (James 2:19). With Satan and his fellow fallen angels having such a history with God and His wrath, they may not be all that impressed with much of our super-great worship services.

The enemy is watching what we do *after* those services. How we live outside the church building will show him whether we are still in prison. Obeying God's instruction will deliver us from the enemy's destruction. Like Peter, we can obey the Lord's way out of Satan's hands and plans.

This is why the Lord is showing us the importance of seeking Him to understand why He touches us. We need more than the emotion of these touching experiences. We need the information. What does the Lord want us to do?

While preparing to hear sermons, we can ask the Lord to help us get beyond the excitement of sermon delivery, so we can focus on the instructions He releases in those moments.

We don't want to be the first ones celebrating great sermons or weeping during wonderful, spiritually-awakening moments, only to be the last ones to show up at Sunday school or Bible study—or not show up at all.

Peter's experience shows us how the Lord prepares people to hear and do His instructions. Let us see how the Lord's touch and instructions get Peter out.

A Time to Rest and a Time to Move

When facing enormous challenges, some people think the best thing to do is to rest in the Lord and let Him take care of everything. They believe He will bring them out somehow.

If God wants us to rest, He will give us rest. However, the Lord might have a plan that requires action on our part. Like the old congregational song says, "When the Lord gets ready, you got to move!"

Snoring when the enemy arrives doesn't prove we have reached some mature level of faith in believing that God will deliver us; getting up and obeying God's instructions does. In other words, we have to participate in our deliverance.

Peter's participation began with waking up. The Lord had decided the apostle needed to get up, get instructions, and get out.

What to Put On So You Can Move On

> And the angel said unto him, "Gird thyself, and bind on thy sandals." And so he did. And he saith unto him, "Cast thy garment about thee, and follow me" (Acts 12:8).

Peter had to get dressed and then put on his shoes and coat.

Like this apostle, many of us have been touched to wake up and get out of our captive places. The time has come for us to experience the manifestation of God's deliverance. We must get dressed for our deliverance experiences.

3

Just as the angel told Peter what to put on, the Lord will show us what we need to proceed. What is the Lord instructing us to put on or add to our characters, behaviors, or spiritual development as He prepares us to follow Him to deliverance?

Let us meditate on and obey His instructions given in these Scriptures:

> *And beside this, giving all diligence, add to your faith virtue, and to virtue knowledge; and to knowledge temperance; and to temperance patience; and to patience godliness; and to godliness brotherly kindness; and to brotherly kindness charity. For if these things be in you and abound, they make you that ye shall neither be barren nor unfruitful in the knowledge of our Lord Jesus Christ* (2 Peter 1:5–8).

> *Put on therefore, as the elect of God, holy and beloved, bowels of mercies, kindness, humbleness of mind, meekness, longsuffering; Forbearing one another, and forgiving one another, if any man have a quarrel against any: even as Christ forgave you, so also do ye. And above all these things put on charity, which is the bond of perfectness (perfect bond of unity). And let the peace of God rule in your hearts, to the which also ye are called in one body; and be ye thankful* (Col. 3:12–15).

> *Put on the whole armour of God, that ye may be able to stand against the wiles of the devil ... Wherefore take unto you the whole armour of God, that ye may be able to withstand in the evil day, and having done all, to stand. Stand therefore, having your loins girt about with truth, and having on the breastplate of righteousness; and your feet shod with the preparation of the gospel of peace; above all, taking the shield of faith, wherewith ye shall be able to quench all the fiery darts of the wicked; praying always with all prayer and supplication in the Spirit* (Eph. 6:11, 13–18).

Going for a Victory Walk Through Enemy Situations

Peter was awakened, raised up, and clothed for his deliverance. He had an angel for his guide. However, the apostle was still in jail surrounded by enemy forces. He would have to walk past wards of prison guards to get out (Acts 12:10).

What do you do when the only way out is to go through an enemy camp filled with demonic forces assigned to capture and destroy you? *Follow instructions.*

Peter had an angelic guide to help him through his walking assignment. The Lord has given us the Holy Spirit to show us the steps to take, especially through the enemy's camp.

There are times when we must stand still and see the salvation of the Lord. However, there are times when we, like Peter, just have to go for a walk. In all cases, God's instructions lead us to deliverance.

He has given us these Scriptures to encourage us in our walking assignments:

> *Yea though I walk through the valley of the shadow of death, I will fear no evil: for thou art with me; thy rod and thy staff they comfort me* (Ps. 23:4).

> *When you pass through the waters, I will be there, through rivers, it will not overflow you. When you walk through fire you will not be burned; neither shall the flame kindle upon thee* (Isa. 43:2).

Walking through areas filled with guards, Peter took bold steps to participate in his deliverance.

Peter received training to do such victory walks from Jesus, who had a way of getting through crowds bent on destroying him. On one occasion, Jesus had to walk through a crowd of people who disagreed with his teachings in Nazareth. They "were filled with wrath" and forced him out of the city, leading him to the edge of a hill. They were going to throw him over headfirst (Luke 4:28–29).

However, Jesus "passing through the midst of them went his way" (verse 30). Jesus is the Word, who knows how to get through.

He can show us how to pass through rejection, grief, loneliness, disappointments, debts, and marital issues.

Jesus knows how to walk victoriously through habits, hurts, oppressions, betrayals, and the challenges of singlehood. He knows how to move us beyond physical, spiritual, and emotional limitations, and anything else Satan tries to use to throw us off the cliff.

When we are on the edge, feeling as though enemy forces will throw us over and win, Jesus is there to show us how to pass through them and walk away in victory.

Remember, after Jesus passed through the crowd, he "went his way" (Luke 4:30). He will show us how to move through crowds and go His way.

In Luke 4:31–32, we see that after overcoming the crowd, Jesus went to teach in Capernaum, a city about twenty miles from Nazareth. The people there were "astonished at his doctrine: for his word was with power" (verse 32).

Not only can Jesus lead us on victory walks through our crises, He will put miles—and years—between us and the cliffs the enemy tries to throw us over.

Jesus will lead us through pain to power. He won't let us stay stuck in captivity. Through instruction, He'll show us how to get out, go His way, and fulfill the purpose He has for us—with power!

Now unto him that is able to do exceeding abundantly above all that we ask or think, according to the power that worketh in us (Eph. 3:20).

Whether the enemy tries to keep us in captivity with an execution plan or attempts to use situations to throw us over the edge, we have the examples of Jesus and Peter to show that we, too, can do the victory walk.

Let Us Pray

Lord, show us how to get free, to pass through struggles, to experience your deliverances, and to continue our lives strengthened by Your power. Lord, show us how to minister with power, encourage someone with power, love our enemies with power, strengthen our families with power, and do Your will with power.

Instruct us, Lord. Amen.

Open, Says God

Peter followed his angelic guide through the prison. They came to an iron gate, the final obstacle standing between him and freedom (Acts 12:10).

Some of us are close to deliverance. We've learned lessons, made improvements, and victory walked through demonic assignments. Now we are at the gate, the one thing standing between us and total, outright freedom.

For many of us, this gate symbolizes the person, relationship, habit, or hurt that seems intimidating and unmovable. To some people, the gate seems to block freedom.

For Peter, the gate was the opening to deliverance. Acts 12:10 shows that the gate "opened to them of his own accord" (Acts 12:10). Peter did not have to steal a key or fight prison guards to get it. He didn't try to squeeze through the gate's bars or climb them. He just followed the instructions that led him to the gate of his situation, and then the gate just opened.

When entering or exiting stores, there are certain areas we must go through for the sensor-equipped doors to open automatically. The Lord knows where we need to be in our situations for us to experience the openings. He knows how we got into our situations and how we're getting out. He knows where our issues started and where they end. He knows where the iron gates of our situations are. He will lead us to the end, and then He'll open the gates for us to experience the freedom and victory He planned for us.

Our testimony should be that God opened the gates and did for us whatever pleases Him. He heard our prayers and answered them. He opened the relationships, healings, ministries, bank accounts, opportunities, promotions, and other situations to accomplish His plans for us.

We do not have to get stuck at gates. They already have God's directions to open. Like Peter, we just have to follow instructions to get to and through gates.

A Vision to Obey

Acts 12:9 provides several interesting details about Peter's escape.

One detail is that Peter thought his experience with the angel was a vision. Peter did not realize his miraculous escape was real until after he had walked through the iron gates. The apostle had been obedient throughout his deliverance process, even when he thought he was simply having a vision.

Like Peter, we can envision ourselves being obedient to the Lord's instructions, and that vision will become real in our lives. Then we will experience the awesome things God plans to do for and through us.

> But as it is written, "Eye hath not seen, nor ear heard, neither have entered into the heart of man, the things which God hath prepared for them that love him." But God hath revealed them unto us by his Spirit: for the Spirit searcheth all things, yea, the deep things of God (1 Cor. 2:8–10).

When we are in trouble, we need the vision of the Lord, who knows what we know not. We must adjust our vision to see beyond the enemy so that our responses will be in line with the presence of the kingdom of God.

Consider the eye-opening experience of the prophet Elisha's servant when an enemy army surrounded them, as told in 2 Kings 6. Israel was at war with Syria, whose king planned surprise attacks that never happened because God revealed the strategic details to Elisha. The prophet told Syria's plan to Israel's king, enabling him to avoid the traps. After becoming aware of Elisha's actions, Syria's king sent his army to get the prophet:

> And when the servant of the man of God was risen early, and gone forth, behold, an host compassed the city both with horses and chariots. And his servant said unto him, "Alas, my master! How shall we do?" And he answered, "Fear not: for they that be with us are more than they that be with them." And Elisha prayed, and said, "Lord, I pray thee, open his eyes, that he may see." And the Lord opened the eyes of the young man; and he saw: and, behold, the mountain was full of horses and chariots of fire round about Elisha (2 Kings 6:15–17).

The Lord opened the eyes of Elisha's servant to see the presence and protection of His kingdom.

The Lord wants us to see His kingdom in every situation. In Matthew 6:33, we have instructions to seek first the kingdom of God and His righteousness—God's way of doing things. Then God will add to our lives the things we need.

Many of us have plans or dreams we want to become reality. There are questions we can ask ourselves concerning our desires: Have we asked the Lord to examine our visions and plans? Did we wait for His answers? Are we asking Him to show us things we haven't thought of having visions about?

> *Moreover the word of the Lord came unto Jeremiah the second time, while he was yet shut up in the court of the prison, saying, "Thus saith the Lord the maker thereof, the Lord that formed it, to establish it; the Lord is his name; Call unto me, and I will answer thee, and show thee great and mighty things, which thou knowest not" (Jer. 33:1–3).*

He "Wist Not"/We "Wist Not"

Another interesting point from Acts 12:9 is that Peter "wist not that it was true which was done by the angel; but thought he saw a vision."

Wist not means knew not.

Then in verse 11:

> *And when Peter was come to himself, he said, "Now I know of a surety, that the Lord hath sent his angel, and hath delivered me out of the hand of Herod, and from all the expectation of the people of the Jews."*

No matter how spiritually experienced we are or how many verses we know, there are times when we may have "wist not" moments like the apostle Peter. We may not immediately know that God is steering particular situations certain ways for His glory and our victory. We may not realize He is closing doors we want opened, establishing relationships we haven't considered, stopping career moves we put into motion, or ending friendships we're trying to keep. We may not be aware of how God is using people to guide us in our times of trouble.

We must be humble enough to allow God to show us what we don't know as He leads us to victory. Like Peter, we will just have to trust God and obey His instructions.

Let Us Pray

Lord, we thank You for using Peter's experience to show us Your power to deliver in dire circumstances. Please show us what You would have us to know about our situations, challenges, and plans.

You said Your thoughts are higher than our thoughts (Isa. 55:8–9); and the thoughts you have for us are thoughts of peace, not of evil, to give us hope and a victorious future (Jer. 29:11).

Lord, give us instructions based on Your knowledge of our issues. You know the touch we need, the chains that must come off, the godly attributes we must put on, the demonic influences we must pass through, the iron gates that must open, and the way we should go after we are free.

Lord, please touch us and empower us to follow your instructions. Amen.

CHAPTER 2

Touched with Bands:
Learning from Ezekiel's Experience

Many of us ask the Lord to use us for great works. We ask Him to anoint us to complete our tasks. As we have seen with the apostle Peter, doing the Lord's work can put us in strange and uncomfortable positions. However, the Lord will not leave us stranded with no strength. He is here to help us overcome our limitations and remain obedient. We must continue to be committed and submitted vessels in His capable hands.

Let us learn from the prophet Ezekiel's experience based on his God-given instructions outlined in Ezekiel 4:1–8. Note what God plans to do to help Ezekiel obey His orders.

In Ezekiel 4, the prophet received instructions on the role his body was to play in prophesying about the impending judgment on Israel and Judah for their sins of disobeying God and worshiping idols. God instructed Ezekiel to lie on his left side for 390 days to mark the years of Israel's iniquity (Ezek. 4:4–5). Then the prophet had to lie on his right side for 40 days denoting the years of Judah's sin condition (verse 6). God "lay bands" (or put ropes) on Ezekiel to keep his body in the commanded sleeping positions (Ezek. 4:8).

Ezekiel surrendered his entire being to follow instructions, and God made sure Ezekiel's body stayed in position to complete those sleeping days. Ezekiel's sleeping experience shows us how God keeps our bodies in position to do His will. Besides having to lie on his sides for a total of 430 days, Ezekiel was told what and how much he could eat and drink and how to prepare his food. This was done for a prophetic purpose, as God wanted to convey His messages to the people of Israel and Judah.

Having allowed God to deal with his body, Ezekiel had a vision of God showing him a valley of dry bones (Ezek. 37). In this vision, God instructs Ezekiel to call life and power to the divided nations of Israel and Judah. The prophet also sees the people transformed from being scattered skeletons to becoming a united God-obeying force, standing together as "an exceeding great army" (Ezek. 37:10).

Ezekiel's experience teaches us that whatever God is calling us to do, we must purpose in our hearts to surrender our total being to Him. James 1:22–25 teaches us to be both hearers and doers of the Word of God.

What is God asking us to do with our bodies? Is He telling some of us to lose weight, move to another location, walk away from conflict, or wear (or stop wearing) certain types of clothes?

We need the Lord to instruct us on how our spiritual and physical beings work together to please Him.

We live in a world where people claim, "This is my body, and I'll do what I want with it." Let us see what God, the Almighty Creator of our bodies, has to say about that:

> *"Know ye not that ye are the temple of God, and that the Spirit of God dwelleth in you? If any man defile the temple of God, him shall God destroy; for the temple of God is holy, which temple ye are"* (1 Cor. 3:16–17).

> *"What? know ye not that your body is the temple of the Holy Ghost which is in you, which ye have of God, and ye are not your own? For ye are bought with a price: therefore glorify God in your body, and in your spirit, which are God's"* (1 Cor. 6:19–20).

While teaching His disciples to pray, Jesus told them to say, "Thy kingdom come; Thy will be done *in earth* as it is in heaven" (Matt. 6:10; italics mine). God, who created us from the earth, wants His will done *in us,* so that He can use our physical beings to carry out His instructions throughout the earth.

We are to worship God with our bodies. This involves more than raising our hands in worship, kneeling at the altar, jumping for joy, ushering people to their seats, holding the collection plate, or meeting other church responsibilities that require physical activity. Every day, we are to present our bodies to God, acknowledging that He has a say in what we do, how we behave, and where we go.

> *"I beseech you therefore, brethren, by the mercies of God, that ye present your bodies a living sacrifice, holy, acceptable unto God, which is your reasonable service"* (Rom. 12:1).

Physical Evidence

Like Ezekiel, there are several prophets and servants in the Bible whose bodies experienced limitations and preparations in obedience to the Lord's will.

- Abraham had to circumcise himself, his male family members, and his servants as a sign of being separated unto God (Gen. 17:9–14).
- Moses washed Aaron and Aaron's sons to prepare them for the priesthood. They received instructions to wear specially made sacred clothing (Lev. 8).
- Samson—living under guidelines of the Nazarite vow— could not cut his hair, imbibe drinks with alcohol, touch dead bodies, or eat certain types of animals. His mother had to observe the vow while pregnant with him (Judg. 13).
- Esther underwent a year of massaging, purifying, and perfuming before becoming queen (Est. 2:12). God used her to save His people from a plot to destroy them.
- Isaiah was told by God to walk around naked and barefoot for three years as a warning that the nations Judah relied on for protection would themselves undergo defeat and humiliation (Isa. 20:2–4).
- Jeremiah wore a yoke around his neck to convince Judah to submit to God's punishment issued in response to the nation's sins (Jer. chapters 27 and 28).

- Ezekiel shaved his head and beard in prophetic demonstration of the punishment and shame an unrepentant Jerusalem would experience in front of other nations because of ongoing sinful behavior (Ezek. 5:1–4).
- A young and unmarried Mary yielded her body to God's plan, becoming pregnant with Jesus Christ through the miracle of the Holy Ghost and delivering the Savior to the world (Matt. 1:18–25).
- John the Baptist wore camel skin and ate wild locusts and honey during his prophetic ministry in the wilderness, where he preached, baptized, and urged people to repent and prepare to receive the Lord (Matt. 3:4 and Mark 1:4–6).
- Hebrews 11 tells of people who suffered physical consequences—including torture and death—because of their uncompromising commitment to God.

Jesus made the ultimate physical sacrifice. As a result, we receive forgiveness of sins, redemption from eternal punishment, reconciliation with God our Father, and eternal life in His kingdom.

> For it is not possible that the blood of bulls and of goats should take away sins … "but a body hast thou prepared me" … Then said he, "Lo, I come to do thy will, O God." … By the which will we are sanctified through the offering of the body of Jesus Christ once for all (Heb. 10:4, 5, 9, 10).

While on earth, Jesus did many awesome things with His body. He extended His hands to heal the sick. He knelt to pray and to wash the disciples' feet. He sat down or stood up to teach. He walked to various places to preach.

However, there was one particular instruction Jesus had to fulfill for our salvation. He had to get His body on the cross. His physical positioning on the cross released us from having to pay the horrifying penalty for sin.

Jesus was beaten and whipped. He suffered other torturous actions against Him. However, He would not die without His body being on that cross. He was obedient to His death and resurrection instructions.

"As the Father knoweth me, even so know I the Father: and I lay down my life for the sheep ... Therefore doth my Father love me, because I lay down my life, that I might take it again ... No man taketh it from me, but I lay it down of myself. I have power to lay it down, and I have power to take it again. This commandment have I received of my Father" (John 10:15, 17, 18).

The Savior's body had its instructions. Don't die from being thrown off cliffs. Don't die from being beaten beyond recognition. Don't die from being whipped.

Die on the cross. Be buried. Be resurrected. Be glorified!

CHAPTER 3

Instructions for Provision

The Lord knows how to sustain us in every situation we face. He also has ways of showing us when we are to give or receive provision. When the Lord calls us to be providers, He will show us how to make sacrifices in our own times of need in order to sustain others.

Consider how the Lord's provision instructions sustained the prophet Elijah and a widow's family during a period of drought and famine that lasted more than three years, as told in 1 King 17.

After Elijah predicted that Israel would not get rain because of idolatrous practices, the prophet received instructions from God to go to a certain brook to get water to drink.

> *"And it shall be, that thou shalt drink of the brook; and I have commanded the ravens to feed thee there"* (1 Kings 17:4).

Obeying the Lord's instructions put Elijah in the exact location to receive a miraculous provision of food. The prophet had to go where God had already commanded the food-carrying ravens to go.

Many times, our provisions have been sent, but we weren't in the right location to receive them. Some of us are spiritually in the wrong location. We may be in the land of bitterness, while the emotional freedom we are seeking is located in a place called I Must Forgive.

Where are we in the midst of our trials? Are we in anger, distress, and fear—or in peace, faith, and worship? Are we at the right locations spiritually, emotionally, and mentally to receive instruction? Are we in humility or in pride?

Many of us are praying for debt-free provisions, but we must ask the Lord whether the dollars we already have are in the right locations.

Are we spending frivolously?

Are we meeting our financial obligations?

Are we faithfully paying tithes and giving offerings?

Like Elijah, we must be in the right locations to receive the instructions and provisions the Lord gives in order to sustain us.

Let Us Pray

Lord, please show us where to go—spiritually and naturally—to receive what You have provided in our times of need. Show us where You have commanded a listening ear, an encouraging word, or a hug of comfort to be provided. Show us where we need to be in prayer, Scripture, fasting, worship, and praise to connect with the provisions and purposes You prepared for us. Thank You, Lord. Amen.

Provision Beyond the Ravens

After his raven experience, Elijah was told to go to Zarephath. God said He commanded a widow there to sustain the prophet (1 Kings 17:9).

Obviously, the widow did not know about this commandment, as she was preparing for her and her son's last meal. Though she had a plan for them to eat and die, she still had enough life in her to pause her death plans long enough to honor Elijah's initial request for water (1 Kings 17:10). This widow was willing to provide water in a drought. She was willing to be hospitable at the driest and most devastating point of her life. She still had enough strength in her to refresh a stranger.

However, before the widow got the water, she had to face an even greater and deeper request. The stranger asked for her last meal, her death dinner. She still did not know she was the one God appointed to keep the prophet alive. God would soon reveal this assignment to her.

Zarephath means refined. The widow was refined, as shown in the level of hospitality she displayed in the midst of drought. Also, the ingredients for her meal—oil and flour—were already in order, ready to be cooked once she collected sticks to make a fire. God made her a provider, though she did not know she had enough to sustain a prophet.

Oftentimes, we have substance, but we don't know how to provide. Thus, the substance is used up without accomplishing its purpose.

Seeking and obeying God's instructions for our possessions, finances, time, and energy will keep us from wasting those treasures on irresponsible relatives, so-called friends, and ill-advised projects. We want to help, but we need the Lord to instruct us on *how* to help.

When the widow obeyed *how* to handle her last meal, she experienced a season of supernatural abundance that enabled her to sustain a prophet. The widow said she had a handful of meal in a barrel and a little oil in a jar (1 Kings 17:12). She had to serve beyond what she saw. In making the little bit of food for Elijah and her family, the widow's focus shifted from her cook-eat-and-die plan to obeying prophetic instruction.

> *And Elijah said unto her, "Fear not; go and do as thou hast said: but make me thereof a little cake first, and bring it unto me, and after make for thee and for thy son. For thus saith the Lord God of Israel, The barrel of meal shall not waste, neither shall the cruse of oil fail, until the day that the Lord sendeth rain upon the earth." And she went and did according to the saying of Elijah; and she, and he, and her house did eat many days. And the barrel of meal wasted not, neither did the cruse of oil fail, according to the word of the Lord, which he spake by Elijah* (1 Kings 17:13–16).

Prophetic Provider

The miracle was not about the food substance the widow had, but about the substance of faith, obedience, and hospitality she had within herself. As long as she was willing to obey prophetic instructions, she would be provided the means to give. In other words, the giver kept getting so she could keep giving.

God shifted her from being a last-meal eater to becoming a long-term provider. God's instructions changed the widow's expectations. While she expected to eat and die, God's instructions were to give and live.

Some of us are just one instruction away from experiencing complete God-directed turnarounds in our most challenging situations. Is there a God-given instruction you have yet to obey? Do you feel God's Spirit nudging you to send a card, invite a relative over for dinner, visit someone, give a certain gift, write a book, get involved in a specific church or community project, or mentor someone who needs guidance and encouragement?

The widow's experience presents us a challenge. Can God use us as consistent providers when we are the ones in dire need? The key word is consistent. The widow was consistent in providing food to Elijah and her family in a specific order every day until the drought was over.

When Elijah first met the woman, she was picking up sticks to use to make fire for her last meal. She had two sticks in her hands. She did not expect to need sticks beyond that day.

However, God said "not so." His supernatural provision plans meant the widow would need more sticks to make more fires. God made sure the prophet and the woman's household ate every day.

No matter how low our supplies may seem, we must keep up with our spiritual and natural responsibilities, while expecting the Lord to sustain us beyond what we have left. Be encouraged. Keep picking up sticks. Keep making fires. Keep giving as the Lord instructed. You will have provision for another day!

Let Us Pray

Lord, show us whom we're assigned to keep alive—to refresh, encourage, and sustain. Deal with our attitudes, behaviors, and emotions so we can carry out our provision assignments. Lord, encourage us to remain prepared and productive as we rely on You to make provision every day. Show us how to be consistent participants in our deliverance. Thank you, Lord. Amen.

CHAPTER 4

Instructions for Two
Part I: God Is "Two Powerful"

For this and the next four chapters, our focus will be on the number two and on how God functions through various seasons, circumstances, prophetic assignments, and teams of people.

The Lord will show us the importance of trusting how He positions us in situations. We do not have to be first to be effective. Rather, we should desire that the Lord position us where He will get the glory.

The foundation for this instructional path was laid in Chapter 3, where we learned about the prophetic experience of the widow of Zarephath. Remember, the Lord told the prophet Elijah where to go for provision. When the prophet met the widow, she had two sticks in her hands. The sticks were going to be used to build a fire for a meal consisting of two ingredients, oil and flour. The two sticks were not much, but still enough to get the fire started. The sticks and the two meal ingredients were enough to help her obey the instructions God gave through Elijah to ensure their miraculous survival during the drought.

Through the widow's situation, we realize that when we are down to our last two, it's up to those two to be in position to be used for miraculous results.

Some of us may have just two dollars, two friends, two relatives we can trust, or two volunteers left in our organizations. We may have two faithful members in the choir, Bible study group, Sunday school, or church.

We cannot give up on the "two" in disgust. We can't wallow in self-pity. This is not the time to be discouraged, but to be obedient to the Lord's instructions. We must continue relying on Him to be more than enough in these situations. God can use the "two" we have to manifest the supernatural provisions He has in store for us.

A Testimony of Two

Sometimes we may have just two types of items or resources we can use for ministry, businesses, or whatever God is instructing us to do.

I remember hearing older saints talk about having only two outfits—one for church and the other for the rest of the week. However, they were powerful soldiers for the Lord and knew how to be rich in faith. They testified that God is a Savior and a Mighty Deliverer, and nothing is impossible for Him.

That is what David did when Israel was facing Goliath and the Philistine army (1 Sam. 17). David testified his way to the battlefield. To convince King Saul that he should fight against Goliath on Israel's behalf, David gave a testimony of how God empowered him to defeat two animals—a lion and a bear. David did not present a long list of victorious experiences. He just testified about two.

If God would help David take down two animals trying to kill sheep, then God would certainly help him defeat a man and an army bent on destroying God's people. In Goliath, soldiers in Israel's army saw an unbeatable giant. But faith-filled David saw a conquerable enemy who despised God and defied God's army.

How do we see our giants—trials, challenges, or troubles? Do these giants defy God's plan for us? Are they beatable, or will they keep us on the sidelines of God-given life, relationships, plans, and ministries in fear?

With his testimony of two victorious experiences, David got the king's permission to advance to the battlefield to face Goliath. David ran toward Goliath, using two items—a sling and a stone—to kill the giant.

Even if we have just two testimonies or are equipped with only two items to face the enemy, we can still run like David to do God's will.

We can be eager to obey His instructions as we focus on His victorious plans. Then we can encourage others through our "two" testimonies.

As we go through the next four chapters, we should keep this thought in mind: Trust God. He knows what to do with two.

Now, let us continue on our biblical "two" journey as the Lord shows us He is indeed "two powerful."

CHAPTER 5

Instructions for Two
Part II: Dreams and Extremes

We begin our "two" journey with Joseph, who went through sibling rivalry, slavery, and imprisonment on his way to becoming the No. 2 leader in Egypt.

Joseph's journey started with two God-inspired dreams, from which he learned he was destined to become a leader among his brothers (Gen. 37). The prophetic dreams became reality despite the hardships Joseph experienced at his Canaanite home with his older jealous siblings, who eventually threw him in a pit and later sold him into Egyptian slavery.

In Genesis 40, we see how God enabled an unjustly imprisoned Joseph to interpret the dreams of two other prisoners—a chief baker and a chief butler, who were part of Pharaoh's staff in Egypt. However, when their dreams actually happened (the baker was executed, but the butler was freed and returned to his job), Joseph was forgotten. This innocent man was still in prison.

Two years later, Pharaoh had a dream, woke up, went back to sleep, and dreamed again. Pharaoh was troubled and called for his magicians and wise men. None of them could interpret the dreams. Then the butler remembered Joseph and told Pharaoh how Joseph had interpreted two dreams in prison. The ruler called for Joseph to reveal the meaning of his dreams.

And Joseph answered Pharaoh, saying, "It is not in me: God shall give Pharaoh an answer of peace" (Gen. 41:16).

Through Joseph, God revealed that the ruler actually had one dream in two parts.

And Joseph said unto Pharaoh, "The dream of Pharaoh is one: God hath shewed Pharaoh what he is about to do" (Gen. 41:25).

Joseph goes on to interpret the dream, telling the ruler that there would be seven years of agricultural abundance and then seven years of famine. God instructed Pharaoh on how to manage the two seven-year seasons. Egypt was to use the abundance of the first seven years to survive the famine of the second seven years.

And for that the dream was doubled unto Pharaoh twice; it is because the thing is established by God, and God will shortly bring it to pass (Gen. 41:32).

Receiving God's revelation and authority on the matter, Pharaoh accepts further instruction that a specifically qualified man should manage the nation through the periods of two extremes.

And Pharaoh said unto Joseph, "Forasmuch as God hath shewed thee all this, there is none so discreet and wise as thou art: Thou shalt be over my house, and according unto thy word shall all my people be ruled: only in the throne will I be greater than thou" (Gen. 41:39–40).

Joseph became the No. 2 leader in Egypt and received Pharaoh's second chariot. No one could make a move concerning the nation's resources without Joseph's consent.

Joseph's name means "May God add."[1] As noted in Genesis 41:45, Pharaoh gave Joseph a second name, Zaphnathpaaneah, meaning "The one who furnishes the sustenance of the land."[2]

Egypt was preparing to go through seasons of abundance and famine. The famine season would be so intense and grievous that the time of plenty would not be remembered (Gen. 41:30–31). However, God gave Egypt Joseph, who was equipped with instructions on how to sustain the country during its years of famine. He also led Egypt's efforts in selling food to foreign nations in need. In other words, "May God add" became "the one who furnishes the sustenance of the land."

Let Us Pray

Lord, You see the famine areas of our lives, areas where we lack strength, encouragement, resources, and wisdom. Lord, please give us the instructions we need to remain plenteous in faith and in obedience. Show us the people you have assigned to help us through our seasons. Thank You, Lord. Amen.

Two Sons, Two Seasons

During Egypt's plenteous season, Joseph married and had two sons:

> And Joseph called the name of the firstborn Manasseh: "For God," said he, "hath made me forget all my toil, and all my father's house." And the name of the second called he Ephraim: "For God hath caused me to be fruitful in the land of my affliction" (Gen. 41:51, 52).

Joseph's testimony concerning the first season of his life is in the meaning of the first son Manasseh's name: "For God hath made me forget."

Joseph had gone through a time of toil, both with his family and in Egypt. Joseph's brothers rejected him. They stripped him of the special coat he received from his father and then threw him in a pit. The brothers told their father, Jacob, that Joseph was dead. However, they had sold him to be a slave in Egypt, where he spent years in prison, falsely accused of attempted rape. He became a leader among his prison mates, but was still forgotten by a former prisoner he helped.

However, the Lord caused Joseph to live through and recover from the adversity and anguish of the first part of his life.

The name of Joseph's second son Ephraim, which means "double fruit,"[3] indicates how the Lord radically changed the second season of Joseph's life.

God caused Joseph to be extraordinarily fruitful in the very place he was afflicted.

Joseph's God-given gift to interpret dreams led him from being a prisoner to becoming second in command in Egypt. He led the nation through a fourteen-year stretch of going from one extreme to another. Joseph also reunited with his family.

Because Joseph depended on God to direct him spiritually and emotionally through the first season of his life, he was able to deal with his family and famine wisely in his second season.

During his reunion with his brothers, Joseph encouraged them to let go of the wrongs of the past. He urged them to move into new beginnings of forgiveness, nourishment, and growth.

> *"Now therefore be not grieved, nor angry with yourselves, that ye sold me hither: for God did send me before you to preserve life ... And God sent me before you to preserve you a posterity in the earth, and to save your lives by a great deliverance Haste ye, and go up to my father, and say unto him, 'Thus saith thy son Joseph, God hath made me lord of all Egypt: come down unto me, tarry not ... And there will I nourish thee'"* (Gen. 45:5, 7, 9, 11).

During the famine years, Joseph's family stayed in Goshen, an Egyptian region. The family grew and their possessions multiplied (Gen. 47:27). Then, in Genesis 50, Joseph again had to speak peace and comfort to his brothers, who were still concerned he might seek revenge against them after their father's death. Joseph let them know his focus was not on the wrong he suffered, but on how God prepared him to sustain them and Egypt during two crucial seasons.

While Joseph's experiences differed from the widow of Zarephath, they both had to allow God to take hold of their devastating situations and make them the ones who furnished sustenance in time of drought and famine. The Lord took their lives from one extreme of misery to another of miracles as they submitted themselves and their substances to His powerful hands.

The Lord is here to help us persevere through our extremes. He will do amazing things for us.

Knowing How

What the widow of Zarephath, Joseph, and David all had in common was knowing how to manage their "twos" as they focused on God in faith. They faced their challenging situations, rather than be intimidated into conceding defeat.

We can learn other valuable lessons on this matter from the apostle Paul, who highlighted his experience in knowing how to handle two extremes. He also outlined two conclusions that helped him remain steady and strong in Christ despite favorable and unfavorable circumstances.

> *"Not that I speak in respect of want: for I have learned, in whatsoever state I am, therewith to be content. I know both how to be abased, and I know how to abound: every where and in all things I am instructed both to be full and to be hungry, both to abound and to suffer need. I can do all things through Christ which strengtheneth me"* (Phil. 4:11–13).

Let us first look at the two categories of conditions the apostle said he encountered through his personal life and public ministry. One category dealt with adversity, as Paul used the words "abased," "hungry," and "suffer need." The other category noted better circumstances: "full" and "abound."

In explaining his steadfastness while navigating through these two categories of conditions, Paul wrote, "I have learned," "I know how," and "I am instructed."

The apostle had developed coping skills gained through discipleship. He became proficient in maintaining spiritual discipline, unwavering faithfulness, and consistent obedience, whether the circumstances were woeful or wonderful.

Paul said he received instructions on how to be effective in every situation he faced.

The First Conclusion: *"For I have learned, in whatsoever state I am, therewith to be content"* (Phil. 4:11)

This contentment is comprised of maintaining a state of satisfaction and fulfillment through the relationship with God and His Word.

Contentment involves submission to the Lord's instructions concerning circumstances.

For example, when Paul asked God three times to remove a thorn from his side, God responded, "My grace is sufficient for thee: for my strength is made perfect in weakness" (2 Cor. 12:9). Paul accepted God's decision and in a statement of contentment wrote:

> *Most gladly therefore will I rather glory in my infirmities, that the power of Christ may rest upon me. Therefore I take pleasure in infirmities, in reproaches, in necessities, in persecutions, in distresses for Christ's sake: for when I am weak, then am I strong* (2 Cor. 12:9–10).

We, too, can settle our minds on contentment statements that will help us overcome challenges we face. When we are trying to piece together issues that seem to be shattered, our contentment statement can be:

> *And we know that all things work together for good to them that love God, to them who are the called according to his purpose* (Rom. 8:28).

Sometimes we may feel at a loss because God's navigation decisions seem more like a maze than a process to lead us to miracles. In this case, our contentment statement can be:

> *But he knoweth the way that I take: when he hath tried me, I shall come forth as gold … For he performeth the thing that is appointed for me: and many such things are with him* (Job 23:10, 14).

Also, consider:

> *"For I know the thoughts that I think toward you," saith the Lord, "thoughts of peace, and not of evil, to give you an expected end"* (Jer. 29:11).

We can adopt a contentment statement such as the following to reassure us that God is with us in times of trouble:

The righteous cry, and the Lord heareth, and delivereth them out of all their troubles ... Many are the afflictions of the righteous: but the Lord delivereth him out of them all (Ps. 34:17, 19).

The Lord has provided contentment statements for people with disrupted or severed relationships and for those who are deeply discouraged and want to give up:

When my father and my mother forsake me, then the Lord will take me up ... I had fainted, unless I had believed to see the goodness of the Lord in the land of the living. Wait on the Lord: be of good courage, and he shall strengthen thine heart: wait, I say, on the Lord (Ps. 27:10, 13–14).

Servants who feel their efforts go unappreciated can focus on contentment statements affirming that God does honor their faithfulness:

And let us not be weary in well doing: for in due season we shall reap, if we faint not. As we have therefore opportunity, let us do good unto all men, especially unto them who are of the household of faith (Gal. 6:9–10).

Being content does not mean we are in happy denial about the feelings or thoughts we experience during hardships. However, we are not to allow our emotions to rule us. We must be determined to hold on to what God is doing and saying. We must maintain faith in His will, words, and promises.

Paul did not allow hardships or enemies to have the final say in his life. God's word was settled in Paul, and Paul was settled in God's word.

The Second Conclusion: "I can do all things through Christ which strengtheneth me" (Phil. 4:13)

Christ—the Anointed One—fortified Paul and kept the apostle on course despite the circumstances. Paul did not function in his own power, but through the anointing, which destroys yokes and lifts heavy burdens. The anointing also empowers those who get weary, so they can go beyond their limitations and produce extraordinary results in accordance to God's will.

Like Paul, we can have faith to believe that because of Christ, we are able to persevere through hardships, humiliations, and sufferings.

When we find ourselves questioning how we will accomplish things or get through circumstances, we must remember that Christ is the ability we need. In Him is the power, the knowledge, and the way. Like the apostle Paul, we can do all things through Christ, not through our self-generated plans or willpower. We must rely on the Master's strength.

Throughout Scripture, the Lord reminds us of the effectiveness of His power:

> But thou shalt remember the Lord thy God: for it is he that giveth thee power to get wealth, that he may establish his covenant which he sware unto thy fathers, as it is this day (Deut. 8:18).

> But we have this treasure in earthen vessels, that the excellency of the power may be of God, and not of us (2 Cor. 4:7).

> Now unto him that is able to do exceeding abundantly above all that we ask or think, according to the power that worketh in us (Eph. 3:20).

Let us receive Christ's instructions recorded in John 15:4–5:

> "Abide in me, and I in you. As the branch cannot bear fruit of itself, except it abide in the vine; no more can ye, except ye abide in me. I am the vine, ye are the branches: He that abideth in me, and I in him, the same bringeth forth much fruit: for without me ye can do nothing."

CHAPTER 6

Instructions for Two
Part III: What God Will Do in a Second

Some of us are called to reconstruct buildings, reestablish relationships, restore ministries, or do complete overhauls on ministries. Others must go through a spiritual renovation process as the Lord—the Precise Potter—corrects their marred ways, making them another vessel (Jer. 18:1–6).

The things God will do the second time around will amaze us. Sin, death, unwise decisions, bad investments, waning attendance, or catastrophic weather events may have caused damage or destruction of our first works, including buildings, ministries, relationships, and finances. While we may seem to be beyond repair, God is calling for a redo. The Lord still has special plans for us.

In Haggai 1, the Lord called for a redo when He commanded the people of Judah to rebuild His temple in Jerusalem. He called two leaders—Zerubbabel, governor of Judah, and Joshua, the high priest—to lead the people in the rebuilding project.

The destruction of the first temple occurred after Babylon defeated Judah. The Lord allowed the defeat because of Judah's refusal to turn from their iniquitous ways despite instructions and warnings given through His prophets.

Now speaking through the prophet Haggai, the Lord assures the people that "I am with you" (Hag. 1:13). Then the Lord "stirred up the spirit" of the two leaders and the people to start the rebuilding process (verse 14). After their efforts began, the Lord spoke through Haggai, saying:

> *"Who is left among you that saw this house in her first glory? And how do ye see it now? Is it not in your eyes in comparison of it as nothing? Yet now be strong, O Zerubbabel, saith the Lord; and be strong, O Joshua, son of Josedech, the high priest; and be strong, all ye people of the land, saith the Lord, and work for I am with you, saith the Lord of hosts: according to the word that I covenanted with you when ye came out of Egypt, so my spirit remaineth among you: fear ye not ... and I will fill this house with glory, saith the Lord of hosts. The silver is mine, and the gold is mine, saith the Lord of hosts. The glory of this latter house shall be greater than of the former, saith the Lord of hosts: and in this place will I give peace, saith the Lord of hosts* (Hag. 2:3–5, 7–9).

Working on this project were two leaders and a remnant, but they had more than enough to complete the temple because the Lord was with them.

The Lord is doing the same thing today for those with rebuilding projects. He is touching us with instructions and encouragement as He stirs us for the work. As we obey His commands, God promises to fill our rebuilt areas with His glory.

We can gain insight of how He works in and through us by reviewing several details about Judah's rebuilding experience.

While speaking to the people of Judah, the Lord referred to himself several times as the "Lord of hosts." He has all the angels, supernatural beings, power, and resources at His command to help His people complete the work He stirred them to do. To encourage His people to rebuild the temple, the Lord also spoke through the prophet Zechariah, promising that Zerubbabel would overcome challenges associated with the project.

> *"The hands of Zerubbabel have laid the foundation of this house; his hands shall also finish it ..."* (Zech. 4:9).

The Lord had spoken to Zechariah through a vision, in which the prophet saw two olive trees stationed on either side of a golden candlestick. Each tree had a branch through which oil continuously flowed. The oil streamed into a bowl connected to the candlestick, keeping the flames alight (Zech. 4:1–3).

In this vision, the prophet spoke with an angel who declared God's plans and words. The oil represented God's Spirit and His unending supply of anointing that would pour out to see the rebuilding project through. The builders were going to be empowered by the Lord, not by their own human abilities or strengths.

> *This is the word of the Lord unto Zerubbabel, saying, "Not by might, nor by power, but by my spirit," saith the Lord of Hosts* (Zech. 4:6).

The angel also revealed that the olive trees with the branches represented the "two anointed ones that stand by the Lord of the whole earth" (verse 14). The Lord commissioned and anointed two leaders, Zerubbabel and Joshua, to bring back into existence something that was gone.

The original temple was destroyed, but the invisible God still desired a visible place where He could meet with His beloved people, receive their worship, and favor them with His glory. The two leaders and the people received their instructions and stirring. Now it was time to get to work.

As builders laid the foundation for the second temple, people who remembered the grandeur of the first temple became dismayed. Temple No. 2 would not be like the first one.

To keep the people encouraged and obedient, God had to adjust their vision. Speaking through His prophets, God asked the people several powerful questions about the project:

> *"Who is left among you that saw this house in her first glory? And how do ye see it now? Is it not in your eyes in comparison of it as nothing?"* (Hag. 2:3).

> *"For who hath despised the day of small things?"* (Zech. 4:10).

What are our answers to these questions?

Some of us are holding up rebuilding projects because we are focusing too much on our visions, our remembrances of how things used to be, and our comparisons between what was then and what we see now.

There are people who have gotten to the point of looking down on or loathing rebuilding projects. They have forgotten that these are God's assignments, so they have become impatient, uncooperative, opinionated, and downright rude during the rebuilding processes. Because they are so focused on themselves, they have caused the rebuilding areas to become atmospheres of dismay, discord, and frustration, rather than places of refreshing, renewal, restoration, and rejoicing.

If we are the ones hurting a rebuilding process, then we need to repent and ask the Lord to correct our vision and touch us again with His instructions for His work.

Sometimes, we can become disappointed because the ministries or projects we are called to redo are not as big or glorious as before. We also can become discouraged because few people are committed to these tasks.

However, those tasks are still God's work. The glory of the Lord will be much greater this time around than what we experienced before. Just as the Lord kept His promise to fill the rebuilt temple with His glory, He will fill our work, as long as we are obedient to His instructions.

After King Solomon led the completion of the first temple, the glory of the Lord filled it to the point that the priests could not minister in it (1 Kings 8:5–13). However, the glory manifested in the rebuilt temple was greater because Christ Himself—the Messiah, the Anointed One, the High Priest, the Prince of Peace, the King of kings, the Lord of lords, and the Lord of hosts—would walk through the temple grounds.

So let us heed God's call to restart the youth ministry, the Prayer and Bible Band, the Wednesday night Bible study, the family business, or other rebuilding assignments He has instructed us to do. While the redo project may start out smaller than the original, the Lord will magnify Himself greater than anything we could imagine. Therefore, we cannot ignore His stirrings. We must receive His instructions and get to work.

Let Us Pray

Oh Lord, we thank, praise, and worship You for Your stirring, encouragement, and instructions to get to work. Thank You for encouraging us as we obey Your call to complete our assignments.

Lord, touch our hearts and hands to do the work. The glory of these redo projects is in Your hands. You know what You are going to do with them. You said, "The silver is mine, and the gold is mine" (Hag. 2:8). Thus, You have the equipment, the resources, and the splendor.

Lord, some of us are few in number—even literally down to two. Help us not to fear, worry, or be dismayed; but to have faith in knowing that You, the Lord of hosts, are with us and have touched us with Your strength.

We will not despise the "day of small things" (Zech. 4:10) but will focus on You, our magnificent and glorious God.

Thank You for touching us with instructions and moving us to get to work, get to work, get to work. Amen.

The Blessing of Being Second

The Lord said that some of us are irritated, upset, and bitter because we wanted first, as in first place, first prize, chairperson, presidency, leader of the board, head of council, and director of specific ministries.

Yes, we wanted to be first, but the Lord placed us second.

What He wants done and how He wants it done are more important than the positions we want to be in to get it done. So cry out to the Lord and say, "Lord, get this anger and self-pity out of me and anoint me to get to work!"

As we submit ourselves to what God wants to do in a second, let us look to Jesus, our great and humble example. In 1 Corinthians 15:45–47, we see that Jesus was the second Adam:

> *And so it is written, "The first man Adam was made a living soul; the last Adam was made a quickening spirit." Howbeit that was not first which is spiritual, but that which is natural and afterward that which is spiritual. The first man is of the earth: the second man is the Lord from heaven.*

The obedience of the second man, Jesus, had to cover the disobedience of the first man, Adam, in the Garden of Eden. Adam sinned by doing his own will, rather than obeying God's instructions not to eat fruit from a certain tree. Jesus—facing the approaching time for his crucifixion—surrendered himself to complete obedience in the Garden of Gethsemane:

> And he said, "Abba, Father, all things are possible unto thee; take away this cup from me: nevertheless not what I will, but what thou wilt" (Mark 14:36).

Because the first man, Adam, did not stay away from a certain tree, the second man—Jesus, our Savior and Healer—had to die on a tree to pay our penalty for sin and to reconcile us back to God.

> For hereunto were ye called: because Christ also suffered for us … who his own self bare our sins in his own body on the tree, that we, being dead to sins, should live unto righteousness: by whose stripes ye were healed. For ye were sheep going astray; but are now returned unto the Shepherd and Bishop of your souls (1 Peter 2:21, 24–25).

The second Adam fulfilled an extraordinary, notable, and celebrated level of obedience whereby all of humankind can receive salvation. Prayerfully reviewing what Jesus did provides us insight on how we are to obey God's instructions.

Consider the humility, responsibilities, work, and depth of obedience God is calling us into in order to do His will to rebuild, restore, reconcile, and redo.

Look at the glory of God that came through the second Adam and through the second temple in Jerusalem.

Remember how God worked through the Zarephath widow, whose family ate second after first feeding the prophet Elijah, and through Joseph, who was second to Pharaoh.

Consider Joseph's father, Jacob, who was a twin with Esau. Though Jacob was born second, God chose him as a leader for His people. He corrected Jacob's character and renamed him Israel. Jacob's family became a nation still known by the second name.

Before his death, Jacob announced blessings and prophecies for his sons. Jacob also prayed for Joseph's two sons, giving the greater blessing to Ephraim, the second-born, rather than to Manasseh, who was the eldest. Joseph tried to stop his father and reverse the blessing order, so that Manasseh would receive the traditional greater blessing as the firstborn.

> *And his father refused, and said, "I know it, my son, I know it: he also shall become a people, and he also shall be great: but truly his younger brother shall be greater than he, and his seed shall become a multitude of nations." And he blessed them that day, saying, "In thee shall Israel bless, saying, 'God make thee as Ephraim and as Manasseh'": and he set Ephraim before Manasseh (Gen. 48:19–20).*

God is our order. He knows our placements. Therefore, we should not be troubled when we are second. We are not losers, and we are not left out. We are victorious. The glory and blessings of the Lord are indeed upon us.

We should rejoice, knowing what God will do in a second.

CHAPTER 7

Instructions for Two
Part IV: Quite a Pair

Numbers do not intimidate the Lord. Having only a couple of people available to do His will does not discourage Him from accomplishing His purposes.

The Lord will anoint two people to face many. He can do mighty things through pairs of people who are willing to heed His instructions to save, deliver, and set free those who need His help.

In Genesis 19, God sent a pair of angels to rescue Lot and his family from impending judgment on two wicked cities, Sodom and Gomorrah. The angels instructed Lot—who lived in Sodom—to flee with his wife and two daughters. When Lot lingered, the angels grabbed his hands and the hands of his wife and daughters, and made them leave the city in accordance with God's instructions (Gen. 19:16, 17). The family received further instructions not to look back to the cities while God destroyed them. However, Lot's wife disobeyed. When she looked back, she turned to salt.

God gave two angels, two parents, and two daughters instructions based on His decision to destroy two cities.

Jesus used the "two" approach with His disciples. After training them, Jesus sent them out "two and two"—by pairs—to do ministry. Jesus gave them "power over unclean spirits" (Mark 6:7), as well as sandals for the journey (verse 9) and instructions (verse 10). While each disciple could take a staff on their journey, they could not take any bags, food, or money. Jesus told the disciples to stay in places offered to them and to leave areas where people would not receive their ministry. They were to shake the dust off their feet as a testimony against those locations (Mark 6:10).

While the pairs of disciples did not have much more to go on, they had power, instructions, and each other. The ministry pairs had to go out in faith. The anointing empowered them to stand their ministry ground no matter what situations came their way or who didn't receive them.

> *And they went out, and preached that men should repent.*
> *And they cast out many devils, and anointed with oil many*
> *that were sick, and healed them* (Mark 6:12–13).

God's anointing supernaturally enables us to achieve extraordinary results as we carry out His plans.

Many of us are facing difficult situations, looking for God to do something extraordinary. However, God's intention is to do the extraordinary through us. Often His assignments seem too big for us to handle. The Lord tells us not to worry. He will not leave us outnumbered or empty-handed. The Lord's presence is with us. He has the instructions and power we need.

Let us choose to surrender ourselves to His will and allow His anointing to empower us for our tasks.

A Pair of Promise Believers

Two spies, Caleb and Joshua, were eager to obey God as Israel came close to reaching Canaan, the Promised Land (Num. 13).

Heeding God's instructions, Moses, Israel's leader, sent a man from each of the twelve tribes to spy out Canaan, including its inhabitants, land structure, and agriculture. Caleb and Joshua were part of the spying group.

After forty days in Canaan, the spies returned, bringing large-sized fruit samples from the land. Two men carried one cluster of grapes. Israel had proof that Canaan was everything God said it would be.

All twelve spies testified, "Surely it floweth with milk and honey" (Num. 13:27). However, ten of them also made evil reports, while Caleb and Joshua had good reports.

First, let us read the evil reports that came from the ten spies:

> *"Nevertheless the people be strong that dwell in the land, and the cities are walled, and very great: and moreover we saw the children of Anak there. The Amalekites dwell in the land of the south; and the Hittites, and the Jebusites, and the Amorites, dwell in the mountains: and the Canaanites dwell by the sea, and by the coast of Jordan ... We be not able to go up against the people; for they are stronger than we ... and all the people that we saw in it are men of great stature. And there we saw the giants, the sons of Anak, which come of the giants: and we were in our own sight as grasshoppers, and so we were in their sight"* (Num. 13:28, 29, 31–33).

Now let us read the good reports of Caleb and Joshua:

> *And Caleb stilled the people before Moses, and said, "Let us go up at once, and possess it; for we are well able to overcome it"* (Num. 13:30).

> *And they spake unto all the company of the children of Israel, saying, "The land, which we passed through to search it, is an exceeding good land. If the Lord delight in us, then he will bring us into this land, and give it us; a land which floweth with milk and honey. Only rebel not ye against the Lord, neither fear ye the people of the land; for they are bread for us: their defence is departed from them, and the Lord is with us: fear them not"* (Num. 14:7–9).

These two men believed in God's power to enable Israel to possess the land, but the people chose to listen to the ten other spies. How could a majority of spies be wrong?

The ten spies were factually correct in detailing the cultural backgrounds, placements, height, and strength of the people. Indeed, giants and several heathen nations were occupying the land God promised. They were not going to leave without a fight. However, these faithless spies used the information to support their personal opinions and to scare the people out of following God's instructions to possess the land and worship Him in it.

The people rejected the testimonies of the faith-filled two (Joshua and Caleb), so they missed experiencing God's supernatural power and His extraordinary results.

Had the people listened to Caleb and Joshua, they would have heard the instructions that came with the men's reports. Within the two men's testimonies were the answers of how the nation would overcome a seemingly impossible situation.

Caleb urged the people to immediately go and get it. God has timing in His hands. There are times to wait on His promises, and then there are times to get up, get moving, and start possessing. Whatever timing God appoints, our mind-set should be like Caleb's. We are going to get what God promised.

Caleb and Joshua also said that if the Lord delighted in (or was pleased with) the people of Israel, He would assure their entry into the land and give it to them.

Like Caleb and Joshua, we must keep our focus on pleasing God and remaining faithful to His will, especially in times when we are outnumbered ten to two, so to speak.

> *For the Lord will not forsake his people for his great name's sake: because it hath pleased the Lord to make you his people* (1 Sam. 12:22).

> *The Lord taketh pleasure in them that fear him, in those that hope in his mercy* (Ps. 147:11).

> *But without faith it is impossible to please him: for he that cometh to God must believe that he is, and that he is a rewarder of them that diligently seek him* (Heb. 11:6).

Caleb and Joshua reminded the people that Canaan was a plenteous place with quality land and flourishing agriculture.

When we are overwhelmed and discouraged, reminders of God's promises can encourage us and keep us focused on completing our tasks.

Many people keep and review notes, illustrations, or taped messages detailing promises and prophecies from the Lord.

While giving their reports, Caleb and Joshua repeatedly tried to get the people to calm down and listen, as a majority of them had gotten upset and disruptive after receiving bad news from the other ten spies.

Some of us have gotten close to attaining God's promise only to hear bad news that caused us great distress. We must relax and let the Spirit of the Lord speak to us and bring peace, hope, and courage to our minds. Our minds need to be touched with God's instructions for these challenging moments. We should reject doubtful thoughts and be "re-minded" through the Word of God:

> *I will remember the works of the Lord: surely I will remember thy wonders of old. I will meditate also of all thy work, and talk of thy doings* (Ps. 77:11–12).

> *And be not conformed to this world: but be ye transformed by the renewing of your mind, that ye may prove what is that good, and acceptable, and perfect, will of God* (Rom. 12:2).

> *Let this mind be in you that was also in Christ Jesus* (Phil. 2:9).

> *For God hath not given us the spirit of fear; but of power, and of love, and of a sound mind* (2 Tim. 1:7).

During their report session, Caleb and Joshua told the people not to rebel against the Lord or fear Canaan's residents. However, the people chose fearing Canaan over pleasing the Lord. This led to them rebelling against Him rather than obeying His instructions.

They ignored the fact that God told them the truth about Canaan and that He would honor the covenant He made with their ancestors to give them the land. The people also disregarded the miracles God had done throughout their journey, including: freeing them from slavery in Egypt, parting the Red Sea to protect them from a pursuing Egyptian army, providing a cloud and a pillar of fire to guide them in the wilderness, and supplying manna and quail for sustenance.

The miracle-working God knew the battles and victories necessary for conquering Canaan:

"For mine Angel shall go before thee, and bring thee unto the Amorites and the Hittites, and the Perizzites, and the Caananites, the Hivites, and the Jebusites: and I will cut them off ... for I will deliver the inhabitants of the land into your hand; and thou shalt drive them out before thee" (Ex. 23:23, 31).

If thou shalt say in thine heart, "These nations are more than I; how can I dispossess them?" Thou shalt not be afraid of them: but shalt remember what the Lord thy God did to Pharaoh, and all Egypt; the great temptations which thine eyes saw, and the signs, and the wonders, and the mighty hand, and the stretched out arm, whereby the Lord thy God brought thee out: so shalt the Lord thy God do unto all the people of whom thou art afraid (Deut. 7:17–19).

However, Israel believed their enemies would defeat them, so they rejected God's instructions and refused to participate in their deliverance.

What or who have we been trusting more than God and His promises? Do we believe along with the majority, even though God provided instructions through two or a few people eager to please and obey Him?

Are we one of the two with good reports that encourage people to move from their wildernesses to their promised lands? Do we know that God can defeat giants, whether they are giant debts, giant health issues, giant marital problems, giant family situations, giant bad memories, giant loneliness, or giant hurts?

Our all-powerful God is not afraid of giants. They will not have dominion over His people, His promises, nor His prophecies.

"Only rebel not ye against the Lord, neither fear ye the people of the land; for they are bread for us: their defence is departed from them, and the Lord is with us: fear them not" (Num. 14:9).

After Caleb and Joshua spoke those words, the fearful and rebellious crowd became angry and demanded that the two men be stoned.

However, the "glory of the Lord appeared in the tabernacle of the congregation before all the children of Israel" (Num. 14:10). God confirmed the reports and instructions of Caleb and Joshua. They and their families were the only group from the first generation of wilderness travelers to get into the Promised Land.

Angry at Israel's overwhelming response of disbelief, fear, and rebellion, God barred the ten spies, their families, and the remainder of the people from getting into Canaan. They died in the wilderness, as God put the Promised Land on hold for forty years. The next generation entered Canaan with Caleb and Joshua.

> *Teach me to do thy will; for thou art my God: thy spirit is good; lead me into the land of uprightness* (Ps. 143:10).

A Pair of Praising Prisoners

Missionaries Paul and Silas prayed and sang praises to God despite being beaten, thrown in prison, and shackled (Acts 16:25).

> *And suddenly there was a great earthquake, so that the foundations of the prison were shaken: and immediately all the doors were opened, and every one's bands were loosed* (Acts 16:26).

There were other prisoners there. Some may have been there justly or unjustly. The point is all their bands "were loosed." Look how God moved in response to the praises of two people! Bound people were loosed because two people were determined to keep their focus on God despite enduring harsh situations. The prayers and praises of two persecuted people were powerful enough to shake the enemy's prison.

> *And the keeper of the prison awaking out of his sleep, and seeing the prison doors open, he drew out his sword, and would have killed himself, supposing that the prisoners had been fled. But Paul cried with a loud voice, saying, "Do thyself no harm: for we are all here"* (Acts 16:27, 28).

The startled prison keeper was going to commit suicide, as he assumed the prisoners had escaped and he would lose his life for letting it happen. However, Paul and Silas were there to stop him. The freed ministers were not free to go. The suicidal prison keeper needed ministry. He needed instructions not to harm himself. He needed to know he was not alone, that "we are all here."

This is why we have to maintain godly integrity when God looses chains off our lives and opens doors for us. We have to know when we are free to go and when we've been freed to stay in the situation so God's work can be completed through us. In these cases, our prayer should be "Thank You, Lord. We are free, but still here. Use us according to Your will."

Though they experienced a supernatural prison break, Paul and Silas remained in the prison situation to minister to the prison keeper and his family:

> *Then he called for a light, and sprang in, and came trembling, and fell down before Paul and Silas, And brought them out, and said, "Sirs, what must I do to be saved?" And they said, "Believe on the Lord Jesus Christ, and thou shalt be saved, and thy house." And they spake unto him the word of the Lord, and to all that were in his house"* (Acts 16:29–32).

Then the prison keeper ministers to Paul and Silas:

> *And he took them the same hour of the night, and washed their stripes; and was baptized, he and all his, straightway. And when he had brought them into his house, he set meat before them, and rejoiced, believing in God with all his house* (Acts 16:33, 34).

Look at the ministry, salvation, and fellowship that resulted from prayer and praise started by two men in a jail cell. In Acts 17:6, unbelievers described Paul and Silas as "these that have turned the world upside down."

Like Paul and Silas, we must persevere, though there may be just one or two individuals determined to pray, praise, study, or minister with us. We are still anointed and still responsible for the work the Lord has called us to do. His anointing will free, fortify, and reinvigorate us to move forward.

Let us receive these empowering words of Jesus and be encouraged, especially in our times of "two":

> *"Again I say unto you, 'That if two of you shall agree on earth as touching any thing that they shall ask, it shall be done for them of my Father which is in heaven. For where two or three are gathered together in my name, there am I in the midst of them'"* (Matt. 18:19–20).

CHAPTER 8

Instructions for Two
Part V: A Word to the "Ones"

There are times when God issues assignments for us to do alone or as the lone leader of a group. However, God's wisdom also shows us when we need partners or co-leaders to complete our tasks.

Receiving assignments from God does not mean we are the ones who will solely lead the effort or do everything on our own. The Lord might have other people assigned to work with us. He may have us ask others to help us lead, as they have the qualifications or skills needed for working through the details of our assignments. We can benefit from being humble and wise enough to acknowledge when we need help and seek the Lord's guidance on the matter.

We have read in Genesis 41 how an Egyptian Pharaoh acknowledged that Joseph was better equipped to prepare the nation for the abundant and famine years God had revealed.

Sometimes people have received God's assignments and then become possessive of them, not allowing others into the completion process. Their true motives are to make sure everyone remembers their efforts.

There is nothing wrong with acknowledging the dedication, hard work, and obedience of project workers. The Bible encourages us to respect and show appreciation for those who labor among us (1 Thess. 5:12, 13).

We also are told to glorify God in all that we do (1 Cor. 10:31), for we can do nothing without him (John 15:5). Remember, His name is greater than all the names involved in our projects or listed in church bulletins.

There are times when the Lord will use us like John the Baptist, the lone voice crying in the wilderness, calling for people to repent and prepare for the coming of the Lord (Matt. 3:1–3). While God may call us individually to do specific ministries, we're not the only ones faithfully serving Him, no matter how lonely the journey may seem. God showed this fact to the prophet Elijah, who was hiding in a cave. Let us review how the prophet got there.

Elijah had just experienced an awesome victory over 850 false prophets that served Jezebel, wife of Ahab, who was Israel's king (1 Kings 18). In a showdown at Mount Carmel against these Baal-serving prophets, Elijah called down fire from heaven to prove that his God was the true God. The flames burned the altar Elijah set up (1 Kings 18:30–38).

Prior to that, the false prophets had set up an altar and tried for hours to get their god to bring fire. Nothing happened (1 Kings 18:26–29).

Elijah killed the false prophets (1 Kings 18:40). However, Elijah ran when Jezebel sent word to him that she was going to kill him. He soon became weary and wished for death. Then he went to sleep (1 Kings 19).

He was awakened by an angel, who instructed him to eat and drink. Elijah ate and went back to sleep. The angel returned and touched him a second time, giving him the same eat-and-drink instructions.

Afterward, Elijah walked farther and lodged in a cave. God confronted him. God asked the prophet why he was there. Elijah replied that Israel forsook its covenant with God, killed God's prophets, "and I, even I only am left; and they seek my life to take it away" (1 Kings 19:14).

God had something to say about that:

> *"Yet I have left me seven thousand in Israel, all the knees which have not bowed unto Baal, and every mouth which hath not kissed him"* (1 Kings 19:18).

After informing Elijah there were many others yet faithful to Him, God gave Elijah instructions to continue ministering. He also told Elijah to anoint a farmer named Elisha to be his prophetic companion, who would one day take Elijah's place as God's prophet to Israel. Elisha left his parents to serve Elijah until God swept the elder prophet up to heaven in a chariot of fire.

Like the prophet Elijah, we can participate in powerful victories and still wind up alone in a cave. For example, we can have powerful ministry moments, oversee completion of big church projects, or successfully negotiate major business deals, and still run into a cave of isolation and self-pity because of the great opposition we endured while completing these tasks. We cannot forget that we are not the only ones going through such challenging experiences.

Elijah's experience reminds us that we must drop that "I, even I only am left" attitude and recognize that God has other people faithfully serving Him. He has assigned some of them to work with us. The Lord will show us how to receive them.

Look, Lord, I'm Serving Alone!

Some of us who say we are working for the Lord have become furious and fussy because "I have to do it all myself while they sit around and …"

In Luke 10:38–42, Jesus taught Martha that being the only busy one didn't mean she was doing the most important thing at the time. While visiting with Martha and her family, Jesus taught whoever was willing to sit and listen. Mary, Martha's sister, was among the listeners (verse 39).

> But Martha was cumbered about much serving, and came to him, and said, "Lord, dost thou not care that my sister hath left me to serve alone? Bid her therefore that she help me" (Luke 10:40).

Martha was sincere in her attempts to provide the best hospitable experience for Jesus, but she wanted Mary's help. This meant that Mary would have to leave the Lord's presence to do some busywork. However, Martha did not need Mary to join her; she needed to join Mary at the feet of Jesus.

> *And Jesus answered and said unto her, "Martha, Martha, thou art careful and troubled about many things: but one thing is needful: and Mary hath chosen that good part, which shall not be taken away from her"* (Luke 10:41, 42).

Remember, God does call us to do some assignments individually. He will help us determine which assignments are from Him and which are our self-generated tasks.

Some of us will have to reevaluate the significance of certain projects we are doing alone. Are these projects God-directed or self-generated?

Have we been pressuring people to get involved? Are we complaining to the Lord about fellow believers' lack of participation? Are we asking Him to make certain people help us?

Is our timing off?

We may be at a time where we are supposed to be resting or enjoying family or fellowshipping with other believers or having devotional time with Jesus. Instead, we are somewhere doing right things, but at the wrong times, so we are left to serve alone.

Are we so concerned about loved ones' responses to family, marital, church, or workplace issues that we don't tell them what's going on or involve them in the problem-solving process, so we're left to serve alone?

Can some of us dare to admit we have personality or behavioral issues that result in us not working or relating well with others, so we're left alone to serve?

Some people want to do ministry their way, and they are asking God to send help. Their real motives are to have Him send people they can boss. Well, God is not going to tell someone to leave His presence and join a bossy busybody doing busywork He did not commission.

Martha was alone and wanted her sister with her on her terms. However, Jesus wanted the sisters to be together with Him on His terms.

While she had some things to learn, there is a wonderful thing about Martha that we cannot overlook: Martha opened her home to Jesus. What a powerful deed, especially in a time when Jesus was facing so much opposition from those who rejected His ministry. Martha made sure Jesus had a place where he could sit down, teach, and fellowship.

Martha just wanted to make sure everything was perfect for her Lord and her other guests. She was trying hard to minister to their needs.

However, the Perfect One was there, and He showed her—and us—that we truly minister to Him when we take time to be with Him and receive His words. Jesus is the best activity we can do.

So let us busy ones stop for a second, as moments with the Messiah await us. Join in with those sitting at His feet. Praise and worship Him. Listen to His words. Do not be too busy to experience the best parts of life, which come from fellowship with Jesus and his followers. As we sit together at Jesus' feet, He will show us how to work with one another, how to not be left to serve alone.

Connected with a Couple of Friends

The apostle Paul spent many ministry moments alone. However, he had several fellow believers who became his close friends, including Aquila and Priscilla, a husband and wife missionary team (see Acts 18).

After meeting Paul in Corinth, the couple—who initially lived in Rome—moved with him to Ephesus. The couple set up a church in their home. They all were tentmakers, using their trade to support themselves. Because Aquila and Priscilla were successful at working together at home, in church, and on their jobs, they were of great benefit to Paul and to new Christians. They eventually returned to Rome, and Paul mentioned them in a letter he wrote to Christians there:

> Greet Priscilla and Aquila my helpers in Christ Jesus: who have for my life laid down their own necks: unto whom not only I give thanks, but also all the churches of the Gentiles. Likewise greet the church that is in their house (Rom. 16:3, 4).

Paul connected with two anointed people who showed their unwavering commitment to God, each other, and His church.

Like the apostle, we can be "the ones" who make room for two—or more—spiritually solid people in our lives and ministries. God will assign to us people like Aquila and Priscilla, who will lay down their own necks for us. They will make sacrifices for us, cry and rejoice with us, bear our burdens, be our confidants, love us despite our faults, and go through persecutions and triumphs with us.

Let us not miss the great ministry work and fellowships God has in store for us through the people He assigns to work with us along the way.

So, for "the ones" who have been touched by the Lord's instructions to make room for two, consider the wisdom put forth in Ecclesiastes 4:9–12:

> *Two are better than one; because they have a good reward for their labour. For if they fall, the one will lift up his fellow: but woe to him that is alone when he falleth; for he hath not another to help him up. Again, if two lie together, then they have heat: but how can one be warm alone? And if one prevail against him, two shall withstand him; and a threefold cord is not quickly broken.*

CHAPTER 9

Instructions for Our Ears

The Lord loves our ears and desires an intimate relationship with them. He wants us to understand the blessings of maturing in such a relationship. While the Lord certainly does not mind us seeking His counsel on various matters, He also wants us to engage in an intimate listening relationship with His voice and His ears. Through this relationship, the Lord takes us deeper into Himself, into His divine nature, desires, plans, and wisdom.

This process involves us putting our ears on the altar, making them an offering to the Lord as we submit our hearing to Him. We allow Him to heal and purify our ears as He molds us into wise, discerning, and obedient listeners.

Let us read Isaiah 50:4–5 and give special attention to how the Lord relates to ears and hearing:

> *The Lord GOD hath given me the tongue of the learned, that I should know how to speak a word in season to him that is weary: he wakeneth morning by morning, he wakeneth mine ear to hear as the learned. The Lord GOD hath opened mine ear, and I was not rebellious, neither turned away back.*

"He Wakeneth My Ear to Hear as the Learned"

There are so many sounds and voices to hear in life. We often are encouraged to listen not only with our physical ears, but also with or to our hearts. The Spirit of God is speaking to us daily—"morning by morning"—as a constant companion who comforts, guides, provides insight and discernment, and reveals God's will for us.

To help us wade through oceans of advice, opinions, and ideas, the Lord brings alertness to our ears to identify His voice and words and to follow His instructions.

> "My sheep hear my voice, and I know them, and they follow me" (John 10:27).

Many of us have heard teachings to give God our energy, time, talent, and treasures. Have we given Him our ears?

There is a wonderful example of ear submission to God in Nehemiah 8, where the people of Judah gathered in Jerusalem to hear Ezra—their scribe, spiritual leader, and teacher—read God's law.

> And he read therein ... from morning until midday, before the men and the women, and those that could understand; and the ears of all the people were attentive unto the book of the law (Neh. 8:3).

Now, let us revisit Luke 10:38–42, where Jesus taught Martha that the good part of fellowship with Him is sitting at His feet and listening to His words, which her sister, Mary, did.

> "But one thing is needful: and Mary hath chosen that good part, which shall not be taken away from her" (Luke 10:42).

Mary chose to be a careful and submitted listener of Jesus. He guaranteed His words would stay with her.

Even Jesus needed someone who would unquestionably receive the words He was giving. While there were many people in several locations who believed in Him, Jesus' words often were met with arguments, suspicion, unbelief, and rejection from religious leaders and their followers. Others just wanted His miracles.

However, Jesus enjoyed taking time to sit and talk to people. He did so with the Samaritan woman who came to the well, where he was resting from a journey, as told in John 4:1–26.

Jesus asked the woman for a drink of water. Thus began a conversation between them about living water, husbands, cultural backgrounds, religious history, and worship. They listened to one another's questions and responses as they worked through spiritual and natural issues. They did not have a confrontation, but a conversation. The more the woman listened, the more revelation she received.

> *The woman saith unto him, "I know that Messiah cometh, which is called Christ: when he is come, he will tell us all things." Jesus saith unto her, "I that speak unto thee am he"* (John 4:25–26).

She heard him loud and clear. His words reverberated within her, and she took off running for town.

> *"Come, see a man, which told me all the things that ever I did: is not this the Christ?"* (John 4:29).

Jesus spent two days with the Samaritans, revealing Himself to them as he did with the woman. He talked. They listened and received Him.

> *And many more believe because of his own word; and said unto the woman, "Now we believe, not because of thy saying: for we have heard him ourselves, and know that this is indeed the Christ, the Savior of the world"* (John 4:41–42).

The Samaritan woman's moment with the Messiah led to a town revival. Jesus had indeed awakened her ear to hear as the learned.

Both Mary and the Samaritan woman gave Jesus their ears, and He changed their lives.

Boot Camp for the Ears

When the Lord wakens us to hear as the learned, He is developing our ears to be disciplined and skillful in listening. This means we will have to go to listening boot camp.

Some of our boot camp experiences may include getting 3 a.m. phone calls from people weighed down with troubles. They just need someone to listen. As listeners in training, God will not allow us to remind them of the time, hang up, sound groggy, or attempt to schedule a more convenient time to talk. We are in listening boot camp, and God wants us up, energized, and listening *now*.

We must remember we are God's vessels. He uses us to accomplish His will on earth and in people's lives. Therefore, if God desires to listen to that person at 3 a.m. and chooses to listen through us, then He'll waken our ears to hear. We will have to handle the assignment with maturity and obedience.

In other boot camp training, we may find ourselves in a series of conversations where others are doing all the talking. We can't get a word in edgewise. In these situations, some of us will get angry, impatient, or hurt. We complain that, "They talked me to death." That is exactly what God wants to happen. Some of us are incessant talkers, so God is allowing people to "talk us to death." Dead people don't talk. Some of us have a nonstop-talking spirit that has to die; then God will have room to make us patient listeners.

> *Wherefore my beloved brethren, let every man be swift to hear, slow to speak, slow to wrath* (James 1:19).

As we continue our listening boot camp, the Lord may direct us to go to different locations where people need anointed listeners. For example, God may impress upon us to go to a certain store. We might think we are there for a good sale, but in Aisle 3 is a man who needs someone to listen. We are trying to shop, and he wants to talk and talk and talk. Turns out, the Lord led us to the store for listening boot camp.

The availability of God-trained listeners is vital today, as we live in a society of bank-teller machines, voice and electronic mail, automated response systems, and facsimiles. However, there are people around us who need to talk to human beings. They do not need our advice, answers, or money. They need our ears.

Many people are hurt, angry, lonely, or overlooked, while others have no one with whom to share their good news or achievements. Can God use us to listen?

Can we listen to someone talk about an experience for the eighth time without saying, "You already told me that"?

Can we allow God to slow down our ears—and our mouths—long enough to let Him show us which repeated stories need our patient attention?

Some people have layers of personality, behavioral, or emotional issues they need deliverance from, and "that story" they keep repeating may provide valuable information as to why they are the way they are.

The Lord can touch our ears to hear beyond their words and discern their inner cries for help, healing, forgiveness, and understanding. Then He can touch our mouths, giving us the tongue of the learned, so we will know how to speak a word in season to those who are weary (Isa. 50:4).

Sometimes, "that story" is a positive and genuine source of joy for the person speaking. Be patient and rejoice with those who rejoice (Rom. 12:15). Enjoy their joy and thank God for hearing and sharing these wonderful moments of gladness and peace.

Let us remember the words of Jesus to do unto others as we would have them do unto us (Matt. 7:12 and Luke 6:31), and let us apply this principle to our hearing.

Also, consider this wise warning:

> *Whoso stoppeth his ears at the cry of the poor, he also shall cry himself, but shall not be heard* (Prov. 21:13).

We cannot forget that we also need people to hear us. Let us sow seeds of good and patient listening; then there will be blossoming and opened ears ready to invest time in us when it is our turn to be heard.

Hearing, Learning, and Discerning

As we graduate from boot camp, having matured in our listening relationship with the Lord, He will "waken our ears to hear" the difference between obedience and disobedience, between truth and deception.

In John 10, Jesus said He is the Good Shepherd (verse 14). He said His sheep know His voice and they follow Him. He also said "thieves and robbers" tried to lead the sheep. However, the sheep would not heed them:

"And a stranger will they not follow, but will flee from him:
for they know not the voice of strangers" (John 10:5).

The sheep are skilled listeners that know their shepherd's voice. When sheep detect that what they are hearing is not their shepherd's voice, they run the other way. Their ears only belong to their shepherd.

Listen to the voice. Does it belong to the Shepherd or the stranger?

In John 18:37, Jesus said, "Every one that is of the truth heareth my voice." Heeding the Lord's truth and instructions will keep our ears from falling for lies and deceptions.

We can learn from the lie-detecting listening skills of the prophet Samuel. He heard beyond King Saul's attempts to justify decisions and conduct not in line with God's instructions.

While facing battle against a large number of Philistine soldiers, Saul made a sacrifice to God, something only priests were to do. He had not obeyed the Lord's command to wait for the arrival of Samuel, who also was a priest (1 Sam. 13:5–12). When confronted by Samuel, Saul tried to use his battle circumstances to justify his disobedience. Samuel responded that Saul had "done foolishly" in not following God's command (1 Samuel 13:13).

In 1 Samuel 15, the prophet told Saul God's command to destroy everything of the wicked Amalekites, who were Israel's enemies. After defeating this enemy army, Saul falsely reported to Samuel the battle results.

And Samuel came to Saul: and Saul said unto him, "Blessed
be thou of the Lord: I have performed the commandment
of the Lord" (1 Sam. 15:13).

Saul used flattery in mentioning how blessed Samuel was of the Lord. The king also was boastful in testifying of his so-called accomplishments. However, what the king was saying and what the prophet was hearing were two different things.

> *And Samuel said, "What meaneth then this bleating of the sheep in mine ears, and the lowing of the oxen which I hear?"* (1 Sam. 15:14).

Samuel heard the evidence of Saul's disobedience and deception.

The prophet again confronted Saul about Saul's rebellious conduct and leadership decisions. This time, the king blamed the people. He said they took the "best of the sheep and the oxen" to sacrifice to God and then destroyed everything else (1 Sam. 15:15). However, Samuel told Saul "to obey is better than sacrifice" (1 Sam. 15: 22). Saul's disobedience brought on drastic results.

> *"For rebellion is as the sin of witchcraft, and stubbornness is as iniquity and idolatry. Because thou hast rejected the word of the Lord, he hath also rejected thee from being king"* (1 Sam. 15:23).

This judgment would not change no matter how much Saul pleaded with Samuel and God.

As we learned through Saul and Samuel's interactions, the Lord has a way of letting us hear the "bleating of the sheep" and the "lowing of the oxen" so we won't be deceived by people who say they are doing His will when they're not. The Lord awakens and opens our ears to hear beyond the statements people make concerning religious- and church-related matters, as well as educational, family, health, relationship, political, and work issues.

As He did with Samuel, God will give our ears revelations about the flattering and boastful words used to conceal deception, disobedience, and lies.

> *Shall not God search this out? For he knoweth the secrets of the heart* (Ps. 44:21).

> *When he speaketh fair, believe him not: for there are seven abominations in his heart* (Prov. 26:25).

He revealeth the deep and secret things: he knoweth what is in the darkness, and the light dwelleth with him ... But there is a God in heaven that revealeth secrets (Dan. 2:22, 28).

Therefore, judge nothing before the time, until the Lord come, who both will bring to light the hidden things of darkness, and will make manifest the counsels of the hearts: and then shall every man have praise of God (1 Cor. 4:5).

Let us be patient and wait "until the Lord come" to reveal the truth.

Some of us have friendships and relationships that feel right, as everything seems to be going great. However, the Lord knows the deceptions and ugly results that lie ahead, so He is telling us to end things now.

Others are considering business and real estate proposals that appear to be legitimate and profitable, with every detail in order. However, the Lord knows which business deals are detrimental to us. He will touch our ears to listen wisely to company representatives and contract negotiators. We also will hear when the Lord's voice comes to us saying, "Don't sign the contract."

Let no man deceive you with vain words: for because of these things cometh the wrath of God upon the children of disobedience. Be not ye therefore partakers with them (Eph. 5:6, 7).

Obedient ears are vital for having a thriving listening relationship with the Lord. We cannot be like Saul, who valued his will more than the voice of the Lord and then tried to sacrifice his way out of trouble.

The Lord wants obedient hearers who are willing to do His words. We can sacrifice time, money, and many other things for God, but He wants our ears on the altar. He wants to clean out the wax of disobedience and self-will that clog the ears.

Sacrifice and offering thou didst not desire, mine ears hast thou opened: burnt offering and sin offering thou has not required (Ps. 40:6).

While we have our own ideas and methods on how to approach the issues of our lives, our ears must humbly bow to the superior and divine thoughts and ways of the Lord (Isa. 55:9). The Lord's voice does not come to our ears to stifle us, but to reveal the obedience He wants from us. His words come forth to bless, counsel, and mature us.

"So shall my word be that goeth forth out of my mouth: it shall not return unto me void, but it shall accomplish that which I please, and it shall prosper in the thing whereto I sent it" (Isa. 55:11).

"The Lord Hath Opened Mine Ear, and I was not Rebellious, Neither Turned Away Back"

Isaiah 50:5 shows us another component of God's relationship with our ears. This involves paying close attention with the commitment to do what He says.

"And why call ye me, 'Lord, Lord': and do not the things which I say?" (Luke 6:46).

But be ye doers of the word, and not hearers only, deceiving your own selves (James 1:22).

In Revelations 2 and 3, the Lord makes seven churches aware of His thoughts, warnings, and instructions concerning them. He ends each address with "He that hath an ear, let him hear what the Spirit saith unto the churches" (Rev. 2:7, 11, 17, 29, and 3:6, 13, 22). The churches could either receive or reject what God revealed.

God opens our ears so His words and will can get into our minds, hearts, and emotions. The more we receive His testimonies in our hearing, the more our faith in Him will grow, our love for Him will deepen, and our obedience to Him will be consistent.

Come and hear, all ye that fear God, and I will declare what he hath done for my soul (Ps. 66:16).

> *So then faith cometh by hearing, and hearing by the word of God* (Rom. 10:17).

Some people practice selective hearing. They can hear God when He tells them to lead ministry groups or start programs, but ignore Him when He tells them to forgive those who have abused or persecuted them.

They praise God when they hear prophesies of the prosperous things He has planned for them, but disregard His corrective words about their character flaws.

They clearly hear the Lord when He speaks of stopping the enemy. However, their hearing fails when He instructs them to stop doing certain things.

While God can touch our ears to make His revealed instructions clearly heard, we have the responsibility to obediently answer, "Yes, Lord." We should honor and welcome His voice like young Samuel was told to do after he repeatedly thought that Eli, a high priest, was calling him (1 Sam. 3:1–18).

Realizing the Lord was calling Samuel, Eli taught him how to respond. Samuel obeyed the instructions:

> *And the Lord came, and stood, and called as at other times, "Samuel, Samuel." Then Samuel answered, "Speak; for thy servant heareth"* (1 Sam. 3:10).

What a powerful and humble response. Imagine the great things God reveals to willing and obedient listeners.

Consider how the Lord showed the essence of His holiness to Isaiah despite this man's faults. God knew Isaiah would repent and heed the call to be a prophet.

> *Also I heard the voice of the Lord, saying, "Whom shall I send, and who will go for us?" Then said I, "Here am I; send me"* (Isa. 6:8).

Another prophet, Jonah, was less receptive of the Lord's voice. Jonah 1:1 starts with "Now the word of the Lord came unto Jonah." Thus, the Lord opened Jonah's ear to hear, but the prophet did not want to obey instructions to preach warning, mercy, and salvation to wicked

Nineveh, an enemy country to Israel. The prophet initially rebelled and ran away. His actions caused life-threatening problems for him and others. He eventually surrendered to the Lord's word, resulting in salvation for Nineveh's people.

Several of us have caused problems for others and ourselves because we heard the Lord's instructions, but rebelled and ran the other way.

The Lord does not want us to go backward or sink into a lifestyle of disobedience. Therefore, He warns us not to be hard-hearted when we hear His voice (Heb. 4:7). The Lord is calling us to acknowledge His voice and open up to Him. An intimate relationship awaits those who do.

> *"Behold, I stand at the door, and knock: if any man hear my voice, and open the door, I will come in to him, and will sup with him, and he with me"* (Rev. 3:20).

CHAPTER 10

Instructions for Hearing the Healer

For many of us, things we have heard have wounded us deeply. Though some of these painful hearing experiences happened years ago, the words still resound in our minds and hearts. These words affect how we relate to people or handle daily responsibilities.

The Lord knows how to reach inside us to dislodge painful words, so His healing words can have residency within us. The words we hear from Him will encourage, heal, protect, and stabilize us.

Psalms 119 has many verses of how God's words uphold us, especially when we are facing adversities. Read these verses aloud and receive the truth you are hearing about the Lord's words:

> *My soul melteth for heaviness: strengthen thou me according to thy word* (verse 28).

> *This is my comfort in my affliction: for thy word hath quickened me* (verse 50).

> *Thou art my hiding place and my shield: I hope in thy word* (verse 114).

> *Plead my cause and deliver me: quicken me according to thy word* (verse 154).

> *Princes have persecuted me without a cause: but my heart standeth in awe of thy word* (verse 161).

Let us receive the testimony of the Lord presented in Proverbs 30:5:

> *Every word of God is pure: he is a shield unto them that put their trust in him.*

Hearing the Way to Healing

A man known as "blind Bartimaeus" sat near a highway begging (Mark 10:46–52). However, his public appeals were drowned out by the commotion of a swelling crowd. Bartimaeus soon learned that Jesus' presence was the cause of the excitement. He cried out for Jesus to have mercy on him. When the crowd told him to quiet down, Bartimaeus cried out bolder and louder.

> *And Jesus stood still, and commanded him to be called. And they called the blind man, saying unto him, "Be of good comfort, rise; he calleth thee"* (Mark 10:49).

Faith-filled Bartimaeus threw off his garment—which publicly identified his blind condition—and went to Jesus (Mark 10:50). They had a brief conversation that led to a miraculous experience.

> *And Jesus answered and said unto him, "What wilt thou that I should do unto thee?" The blind man said unto him, "Lord, that I might receive my sight." And Jesus said unto him, "Go thy way; thy faith hath made thee whole." And immediately he received his sight, and followed Jesus in the way* (Mark 10:51–52).

Though Bartimaeus's condition prevented him from actually seeing Jesus heal people, he had heard the testimonies about Jesus' healing abilities. Having received faith-building words about Jesus' ministry, Bartimaeus knew Jesus was indeed a healer. Therefore, he cried out to Jesus in faith.

We also need to fill our ears with faith-building testimonies of the Lord. We can achieve this through reading and studying the Scriptures and fellowshipping with faith-filled and encouraging Christians. We can listen to music honoring the Lord and to testimonies from those who had healing experiences with Him.

We need to hear good news about the Lord and about His compassion and love for us. Ephesians 5:19 also tells us to "be filled with the Spirit; speaking to yourselves in psalms and hymns and spiritual songs, singing and making melody in your heart to the Lord."

During his healing moment with Jesus, Bartimaeus immediately received his sight after hearing that his faith had made him whole (Mark 10:52).

Faith is established and increased by hearing the word of God (Rom. 10:17). By faith, we can hear the way to inner healing as the Lord carries us through our sorrows to His joy.

> *Why art thou cast down, O my soul? And why art thou disquieted within me? Hope thou in God: for I shall yet praise him, who is the health of my countenance, and my God* (Ps. 42:11).

> *And I said, "This is my infirmity: but I will remember the years of the right hand of the most High. I will remember the works of the Lord: surely I will remember thy wonders of old. I will meditate also of all thy work, and talk of thy doings"* (Ps. 77:10–12).

> *Remember his marvelous works that he hath done, his wonders, and the judgments of his mouth* (1 Chron. 16:12).

> *"These things have I spoken unto you, that my joy might remain in you, and that your joy might remain full"* (John 15:11).

Because of the depths of their pain, many people have become more committed to hearing the words of their wounds than receiving the healing words and works of the Lord. However, they can learn through Bartimaeus's experience how to shift their focus from their conditions to the Healer.

After hearing about the presence of Jesus, Bartimaeus switched from begging people to give him something to crying out to Jesus for healing.

Our focus, words, and vocal strength must shift from begging people to accept or give to us, to crying out, "Lord, have mercy on us!" Like Bartimaeus, we must value the Lord's presence above what we think we should get from others.

Notice that Bartimaeus did not use his blind condition to get more money out of the large crowd surrounding Jesus. The people were there because of Jesus, not to give Bartimaeus money. He did not need more money. He needed to be healed.

Many of us are hurting. We don't need more stuff to make us feel better. We need healing. We need Jesus.

Determined not to miss his healing moment, Bartimaeus unashamedly cried out for Jesus. He would not let the crowd intimidate him into quietness. As a result, he was able to reach Christ despite the crowd. He could not see to navigate through the crowd, but his voice reached the Lord.

> *In my distress, I called upon the Lord, and cried unto my God: he heard my voice out of his temple, and my cry came before him, even into his ears* (Ps. 18:6).

> *The eyes of the Lord are open upon the righteous, and his ears are open unto their cry … The righteous cry, and the Lord heareth, and delivereth them out of all their troubles* (Ps. 34:15, 17).

> *Then they cry unto the Lord in their trouble, and he saveth them out of their distresses. He sent his word, and healed them, and delivered them from their destructions* (Ps. 107:19–20).

> *"Call unto me, and I will answer thee, and shew thee great and mighty things, which thou knowest not"* (Jer. 33:3).

Bartimaeus cried out, and a moving Jesus stood still. The Healer directed the crowd to call Bartimaeus to him. Bartimaeus had an intimate moment with Jesus in the midst of a crowd.

We can have an intimate relationship with the Lord despite the crowds of work, family, and financial responsibilities, or crowds of physical, psychological, or medical conditions. We can cry out to the Lord, knowing He hears us and has instructions for the crowds and for our conditions. His healing and peaceful presence is here to minister to us.

Be of good comfort, rise; he calleth thee (Mark 10:49).

Healed to Hear Again

Then Simon Peter having a sword drew it, and smote the high priest's servant, and cut off his right ear. The servant's name was Malchus (John 18:10).

And Jesus answered and said, "Suffer ye thus far." And he touched his ear, and healed him (Luke 22:51).

Malchus was a high priest's servant who was—as the saying goes—just doing his job. He was among several men and officers sent by religious leaders to arrest Jesus.

The Scriptures do not indicate whether Malchus agreed or disagreed with the arrest orders. However, his duties put him in a situation where he got hurt.

There were two connections made to Malchus's ear on the night of Jesus' arrest in the Garden of Gethsemane. The first connection was a sword; the second was a touch.

Yes, Malchus was on the wrong side of the situation. However, that did not give Peter the right to cut off the man's ear.

A disciple of Jesus, Peter obviously was on the right side of the issue. Of course, Peter wanted to protect innocent Jesus. However, he was wrong in how he interacted with Malchus.

Jesus admonished Peter and healed Malchus.

Several of us are hurting from the words and actions of those who were on the right side of issues. Their tongues were like swords cutting our ears with impatient and painful words, screams, and cold voice tones.

Some of us avoid, ignore, and hang up on certain people because we cannot stand to hear any more from them.

Like Malchus—who had his ear cut off in a garden amidst a crowd of people—some of us have been publicly humiliated and wounded by relatives, so-called friends, religious leaders, strangers, employers, and enemies. Rather than show us the correct ways, they lashed out and condemned us, using our wrongs to justify their words and actions.

However, Jesus is here to deliver us.

> *For God sent not his Son into the world to condemn the world; but that the world through him might be saved* (John 3:17).

As He did with Malchus, Jesus desires to touch and heal our ears to hear again.

Seeing Malchus's name and ear incident recorded in the Bible shows us that the details of our pain matter to Jesus. He knows about our cut ears. He knows who did the cuttings, where and under what circumstances the cuttings occurred, the instruments used, and who was there.

For Malchus, the Garden of Gethsemane was the place where he was hurt and healed. He received Jesus' touch of healing, forgiveness, mercy, and compassion.

There is healing in forgiveness. We must forgive those who hurt us and trust the Lord to deal with them about their swords.

When Jesus heals us to hear again, He places our ears back in commission as we focus on the Healer's touch, rather than hurtful words. We grow stronger in our hearing relationship with the Lord by listening to His Spirit and receiving His wisdom for our situations.

> *Howbeit when he, the Spirit of truth, is come, he will guide you into all truth: for he shall not speak of himself; but whatsoever he shall hear, that shall he speak: and he will shew you things to come* (John 16:13).

With healed ears, we can become better listeners than we were before our painful experiences. We will be able to hear the Lord's call to minister uplifting words that will heal other people's cutoff ears. We can tell others how Jesus healed us to hear again. We each can proclaim, "I have victorious ears!"

We also will hear and readily obey Jesus' instructions to put down our own swords. We know what swords can do.

> *There is that speaketh like the piercings of a sword: but the tongue of the wise is health (Prov. 12:18).*

Hearing After the Healing

There are times when Jesus healed people in one place, then told them where to go from there. Some people obeyed; others did not.

While we are excited and thankful to be touched by the Lord, we must make sure we are hearing after the healing in order to move in the right direction.

In Mark 2:1–12, Jesus gave after-healing instructions to a paralyzed man.

Moments before this healing, Jesus was teaching in someone's home when four men uncovered the roof and lowered the man to Jesus. After healing the man, Jesus told him to go home.

Several people, including religious leaders, grumbled at this healing because Jesus declared the man's sins forgiven. They did not believe Jesus had the right to forgive sins. They cared less about the man's healing. Rather than have the healed man remain the focus of other people's issues, Jesus sent him home. In Mark 2:12, we see that the man immediately got up, picked up his bed, and left.

That is what some of us need to do—get healed and go home. We don't need to get into debates with people who don't agree with how the Lord forgives, touches, or heals us. We need to go home to God's presence and His word. Go home to prayer, praise, and peace. We had sins; the Lord forgave us. We were hurt; the Lord healed us. So, rejoice in the Lord, thank Him for His goodness, and go home!

In another healing situation, Jesus cured a man with leprosy and told him to keep silent about the experience (Mark 1:40–45). Jesus also told the man to show the priest this healing and give an offering to God according to the commandments of Moses. Jesus' healing and the priest's confirmation meant the previously isolated man would be welcomed back into society.

The man received great healing, but did not heed Jesus' instructions.

> *But he went out, and began to publish it much, and to blaze abroad the matter, insomuch that Jesus could no more openly enter into the city; but was without in desert places: and they came to him from every quarter* (Mark 1:45).

The man handled the testimony according to his will.

Like this leprosy-free man, some people have amazing healing experiences and are more than eager to share them. However, they have not allowed the Lord to instruct them about their testimonies; thus, the focus of their testimony shifts from Him to them. Now they are the stars of the testimonies as they "publish it much" and "blaze abroad the matter."

Jesus knows how our testimonies will affect others, His ministry, and us. Due to this man's disobedience, Jesus could not do ministry in the city the way He wanted. Jesus desired to teach and preach to the people, to bring them into the kingdom of God through repentance and salvation.

However, the people only had interest in Jesus' healing abilities. They went after Him focused on what they wanted to get from Him, rather than on receiving what He wanted to give.

Even today, many people make decisions on how they will relate to the Lord, rather than allowing Him to minister salvation, healing, and instructions to them according to His will. They only see Jesus as a healer, rescuer, or provider. They come to Him with their wish lists instead of their lives.

When they are in trouble, they start coming to worship and prayer services and Bible studies. They seek prayer and counsel from saved family members. They start paying tithes or giving sacrificial offerings. Then when their crises are over, they're done with Jesus.

Some people develop these "get-me-out-of-trouble" approaches to Jesus' ministry because they hear testimonies not given according to the Lord's will. While the testifiers meant well in sharing their experiences, their testimonies did not yield the results the Lord desired from the hearers.

The Lord can use obedient testifiers who will lay their testimonies at His feet and let Him instruct them on when, where, and how to share these experiences. The key is to let Him tell us how to talk about Him. Then hearers will focus on the unlimited greatness of the Lord and will be encouraged to surrender themselves completely to Him.

For example, the Lord directed the testimony of a man He delivered from demonic possession, as told in Mark 5:1–20.

After his healing, the man wanted to go with Jesus. However, Jesus instructed the man to go home and tell friends the great things the Lord had done for him and how the Lord had compassion on him (Mark 5:19). The newly healed man became an obedient listener and testifier, obeying instructions as to where to go, who to go to, and what to say.

> *And he departed, and began to publish in Decapolis how great things Jesus had done for him: and all men did marvel* (Mark 5:20).

Let Us Pray

Lord, thank You for touching and healing our ears and opening them to receive Your instruction and wisdom. We yield our ears to You as Your Spirit teaches us how to hear according to Your will. We repent of all hearing sins as we commit to a listening relationship with You.

We receive Your forgiveness as we forgive those who have hurt us. We also pray that You heal the people we've hurt. Our desire is that they forgive us. Lord, help us to forgive ourselves.

Thank you for loving our ears. In Jesus' name we pray, Amen.

CHAPTER 11

Tongues Touched with Instructions

The Lord created the tongue to worship Him and give testimony of His greatness. Around His throne are heavenly beings continuously singing and speaking of His glory. On the earth, He has given our tongues instructions to be instruments of His praise, ministry, and love.

Oftentimes in speaking about the tongue, we focus on God's warning about how sinful and destructive it can be.

James 3:1–9 has become a well-known scriptural source on this topic, and we will review some of its verses.

Proverbs gives wisdom and warning of the depth of damage foolish, proud, and unruly tongues can do. We also will review several verses from Proverbs 15.

In addition, there are scriptures showing us ways the tongue—and mouth—can express good things and thankfulness to the Lord.

> *And my tongue shall speak of thy righteousness and of thy praise all the day long (Ps. 35:28).*

> *Let no corrupt communication proceed out of your mouth, but that which is good to the use of edifying, that it may minister grace to the hearers ... But be filled with the Spirit; speaking to yourselves in psalms and hymns and spiritual songs, singing and making melody in your heart to the Lord, giving thanks always for all things unto God*

and the Father in the name of our Lord Jesus Christ (Eph. 4:29 and 5:18–20).

The Ministry of God's Words

The words of the Lord are pure words: as silver tried in a furnace of earth, purified seven times (Ps. 12:6).

We can trust in God's words. There are no wrong motives or ill will attached to them. God's words are pure, powerful, soothing, and sweet. They are undefeatable, undeniable, and unmovable.

The Lord lovingly and protectively envelops us in His words.

No one can ever go where God is and bring down His words. Many people, species, and elements in the world have come and gone, but God's words stand firm from generation to generation.

For ever, O Lord, thy word is settled in heaven (Ps. 119:89).

The grass withereth, the flower fadeth: but the word of our God shall stand for ever (Isa. 40:8).

God's words are blessings that rain on us and reign in us. His words refresh our minds, hearts, and bodies. The Lord develops an intimate relationship with us as His words go meticulously and surgically into the core of our being. His words have access to every part of us, examining the roots of our thoughts, motives, and decisions.

For the word of God is quick, and powerful, and sharper than any twoedged sword, piercing even to the dividing asunder of soul and spirit, and of the joints and marrow; and is a discerner of the thoughts and intents of the heart (Heb. 4:12).

Through His words, the Lord deals with who we are, why we are the way we are, and His purpose for creating us. His words go to our minds, washing away the painful effects of bad memories and bringing healing and calm as He imparts His thoughts. Through His words, the Lord expresses His love for us and calls us closer to Him.

The Lord has appeared of old unto me, saying, "Yea, I have loved thee with an everlasting love: therefore with loving kindness have I drawn thee" (Jer. 31:3).

The Lord's verbal kindness toward us establishes how we are to relate to others. We can show verbal kindness by giving compliments and speaking gently and calmly; or by being consistent in saying "Please," "Thank you," or "I appreciate you for helping me."

There are people among us who are in dire need of verbal blessings of positive, sincere, and kind words.

Let us be reminded of the difference kind words make in people's lives:

Heaviness in the heart of man maketh it stoop: but a good word maketh it glad (Prov. 12:25).

Pleasant words are as a honeycomb, sweet to the soul, and health to bones (Prov. 16:24).

Lord of the Tongue

The Lord shall cut off all flattering lips, and the tongue that speaketh proud things: who have said, "With our tongue will we prevail: our lips are our own: who is the Lord over us?" (Ps. 12:3, 4).

The Lord of the tongue knows the motives behind the words flowing from our mouths. He knows whether words are generated by pride, false intentions, or humility.

The Lord established this truth in heaven, where battle ensued after an angel named Lucifer decided he wanted a throne above God. Lucifer and his followers—a third of the angels—lost the battle. God kicked them out of heaven.

I beheld Satan as lightning fall from heaven (Luke 10:18).

Consider the pride-filled words Lucifer formed in his heart before waging war against God:

> *How art thou fallen from heaven, O Lucifer, son of the*
> *morning! how art thou cut down to the ground, which*
> *didst weaken the nations! For thou hast said in thine heart,*
> *"I will ascend into heaven, I will exalt my throne above*
> *the stars of God: I will sit also upon the mount of the*
> *congregation, in the sides of the north: I will ascend above*
> *the heights of the clouds; I will be like the most High." Yet*
> *thou shalt be brought down to hell, to the sides of the pit*
> (Isa. 14:12–15).

We cannot allow pride to develop within us and then use our tongues to express itself and its ungodly intentions. Rather, our tongues must humbly bow down to the Lord.

In Daniel 4, King Nebuchadnezzar had a tongue-humbling experience after ignoring a God-given dream warning him to let go of his proud words and behavior. Instead, the Babylonian king continued with his proud ways.

> *The king spake, and said, "Is not this great Babylon, that I*
> *have built for the house of the kingdom by the might of my*
> *power, and for the honour of my majesty?" While the word*
> *was in the king's mouth, there fell a voice from heaven,*
> *saying, "O king Nebuchadnezzar, to thee it is spoken; The*
> *kingdom is departed from thee"* (Dan. 4:30–31).

Notice how the voice of the Lord overtook Nebuchadnezzar's words. God would make the king confess that "the most High ruleth in the kingdom of men, and giveth it to whomsoever he will" (Dan. 4:32).

After the Lord spoke, Nebuchadnezzar's season of humiliation began as he "was driven from men, and did eat grass as oxen, and his body was wet with the dew of heaven, till his hairs were grown like eagles' feathers, and his nails like birds' claws" (Dan. 4:33).

The king remained that way for seven years. Then he finally lifted his eyes toward heaven to honor the Lord as the "most High" with an ever-powerful, everlasting kingdom (Dan. 4:34). Nebuchadnezzar praised and blessed the Lord. The king acknowledged that the Lord is unstoppable and answers to no one as He does His will (Dan. 4:34–35).

Nebuchadnezzar's condition and life changed after his once-proud heart and tongue humbly declared the greatness and Lordship of the "King of heaven."

> *"At the same time my reason returned unto me; and for the glory of my kingdom, mine honour and brightness returned unto me; and my counsellors and my lords sought unto me; and I was established in my kingdom, and excellent majesty was added unto me. Now I Nebuchadnezzar praise and extol and honour the King of heaven, all whose works are truth, and his ways judgment: and those that walk in pride he is able to abase"* (Dan. 4:36–37).

We all must give up every proud word and submit our mouths to the Lord of the tongue. We cannot hide our motives from Him. He knows the activities of our bodies, thoughts of our minds, and words of our mouths. As He did with Lucifer and Nebuchadnezzar, the Lord will hold us responsible for our words.

> *O Lord, thou hast searched me, and known me. Thou knowest my downsitting and mine uprising, thou understandest my thoughts afar off. Thou compasseth my path and my lying down, and art acquainted with all my ways. For there is not a word in my tongue, but, lo, Lord, thou knowest it altogether* (Ps. 139:1–4).

> *"But I say unto you, That every idle word that men shall speak, they shall give account thereof in the day of judgment. For by thy words thou shalt be justified, and by thy words thou shalt be condemned"* (Matt. 12:36–37).

Let us acknowledge our verbal shortcomings and turn to the Lord of the tongue for correction, instruction, and restoration.

We can begin with the prayer of Psalm 19:14:

> *Let the words of my mouth, and the meditation of my heart, be acceptable in thy sight, O Lord, my strength, and my redeemer.*

Words Acceptable and Unacceptable

The Lord has various ways of responding to words we speak in reaction to His decisions and revelations.

Daniel's words were acceptable in the Lord's sight, as Daniel confessed Judah's sins. Daniel asked for forgiveness and mercy. He petitioned God for Israel's deliverance from Babylon's captivity.

The Lord sent His angel Gabriel with a touch and a message.

> *Yea, whiles I was speaking in prayer, even the man Gabriel, whom I had seen in a vision at the beginning, being caused to fly swiftly, touched me about the time of the evening oblation. And he informed me, and talked with me, and said, "O Daniel, I am now come forth to give thee skill and understanding"* (Dan. 9:21, 22).

Gabriel also touched Daniel during an earlier vision. At that time, Daniel had been in a deep sleep with his face toward the ground, and Gabriel made him stand up (Dan. 8:18).

The Lord touches us in many ways, spiritually setting us upright to receive His visions and to give us the skills and understanding we need. His commandment has already gone out concerning us. He has answers, insights, and instructions for all the prayers and situations we bring before Him.

While the Lord does speak to us privately, He also sends messages through ministers, loved ones, children, and strangers. We must be receptive to the Lord's messages and messengers and be careful to respond with words that are acceptable to Him.

Some people respond with words the Lord deems unacceptable. He has ways of quieting them until He has fulfilled His purposes and promises. A priest in Judah named Zacharias had his speaking abilities halted for a period because he spoke unacceptable words in response to the Lord's message.

Zacharias was performing temple duties when Gabriel visited him. This same Gabriel spoke to Daniel hundreds of years before appearing to the priest. The angel conveyed God's promise that a son would be born to Zacharias and his wife, Elisabeth (Luke 1:13). Gabriel also revealed the child's name, John. He gave details of how to raise John because of his calling to prepare people to receive the coming Messiah.

However, Zacharias focused so much on him and his wife being elderly, he expressed doubts about God's promise.

In response to the priest, Gabriel announced another promise:

> *"And behold, thou shalt be dumb, and not be able to speak, until the day that these things shall be performed, because thou believest not my words, which shall be fulfilled in their season"* (Luke 1:20).

The Lord had already announced His promise and plans about Zacharias and Elisabeth's child. Rather than saying, "Yes, Lord," Zacharias added his own words about the situation, so the Lord took away the priest's speech.

Indeed, the Lord revealed His words to Zacharias in a surprising way. The priest was understandably afraid. It's important to note that while greeting Zacharias, Gabriel identified himself and told how he stands in the presence of God and was sent to give "glad tidings" (Luke 1:19). Gabriel told Zacharias not to fear because the Lord had heard the prayers of him and his wife and would give them a son.

However, Zacharias did not respond joyfully or thankfully. Instead, his reactions went from fear to doubt.

The more faithlessness is expressed, the deeper doubt sets in.

Gabriel had to put a stop to this spiritual descent. The angel could not allow doubt to spread to Zacharias's wife, who was to carry the promised child in pregnancy. The child would be filled with the Holy Ghost while he was yet in Elisabeth's womb, so there was no room for inner doubt.

Despite his silencing, Zacharias remained the Lord's priest and continued working in the temple. Then John was born. Relatives and neighbors rejoiced and called him Zacharias (Luke 1:59). However, Elisabeth, choosing to follow God's instructions, told them the infant's name was John (verse 60). This naming decision was outside the tradition of giving a male child the father's name or a family name. No one in the family had the name John.

The group turned to the child's father for the naming decision (verse 62). Zacharias wrote "His name is John" on a writing tablet (verse 63).

> *And his mouth was opened immediately, and his tongue loosed, and he spake and praised God* (Luke 1:64).

After that, Zacharias was filled with the Holy Ghost and began to prophesy. He blessed the Lord and began to say what the Lord had revealed about the child (Luke 1:67–79). Zacharias spoke at home the things Gabriel told him months before in the temple.

Remember, Zacharias's tongue troubles happened in the temple, where he was doing work for the Lord. He expressed unacceptable words while the Lord's messenger was speaking.

How many of us have expressed doubt in church while doing the Lord's work or even while He was speaking? How many of us have added our words to situations after the Lord had already spoken His promise or revealed what He was going to do?

The Lord's words are here for us. Our words must bow down and bow out of the issue.

> *Add thou not unto his words, lest he reprove thee, and thou be found a liar* (Prov. 30:6).

Our self-generated words come nowhere near His powerful, glorious, and awesome words. We must let Him say what He wants to say to us. We must be quiet and receive His words with humility and faithfulness.

Have you ever gone to people with glad tidings you received from the Lord only to have them verbally slap their doubts all over your good news? Many of us who are bothered by such verbal behavior are also guilty of it. We need to admit we are habitual doubt expressers.

While we may not lose our speech like Zacharias, the Lord may touch our schedules so we will not have time or opportunities to talk to certain people about certain things. The Lord may not allow us to be involved in certain church projects because our doubts are speaking louder and working harder than the faith, gifts, and talents needed to complete the tasks. We may start seeing our wonderful ideas fall flat in several situations as the Lord is planning to reveal His words, wisdom, and promises.

The Lord does not allow these things to happen to punish us, but to get our attention. He desires to minister to the areas of our doubts and to fill our hearts, minds, and mouths with His words. The Lord is merciful, forgiving, and loving. While He has already promised to bless us, He also will correct our mouths and tongues so we can receive His "glad tidings" with joy and faith.

Then, like Zacharias, our tongues will be loosed to express acceptable words in the Lord's sight and to people around us.

Homework for the Tongue

Sadly, many of us display godly verbal behavior in public, but not at home. We often forget the Lord sees and hears our speech patterns at home. He wants to remove the ungodly ways of our tongues.

As Abraham started the circumcision process with himself, we must begin the flesh-removing process with ourselves.

The Lord instituted circumcision as a sign of covenant between Him and Abraham (Gen. 17:10–14). The Lord had promised to make Abraham a father of many nations and to give him land where he and his descendants were to live. At the Lord's command, Abraham circumcised himself and then the males in his household, including servants (Gen. 17:23–27). Circumcision continued throughout the generations.

Through prophets, the Lord explained that circumcision symbolized the removing of fleshly ways—or ungodly characteristics—as the people were to be consecrated unto Him. Again, this started with Abraham first going through circumcision at home.

We must surrender our mouths to the Lord of the tongue so He may instruct us on how to speak correctly at home.

> I will behave myself wisely in a perfect way. O when wilt thou come unto me? I will walk within my house with a perfect heart (Ps. 101:2).

Home is the first place we need to demonstrate godly tongue behavior. In our homes are the people of covenant, people given promises of being loved, honored, respected, obeyed, provided for, and protected. Many of us feel we have kept these promises as those in our household have benefited from our financial and material provisions. We work, pay bills, and put food on the table and gas in the car. However, we are not giving ourselves to our spouses or children, resulting in lack of family time and no development of beneficial relationships.

Our actions or lack of proper involvement at home can lead to breakdowns in household communication. Then we use the wrong words or tones to resolve these issues.

There are people who do a full day's work and then rush to do church or community projects or go to board meetings. They readily offer their skills, assistance, and perfect verbal behaviors to these outside endeavors. However, when they are asked to help inside their homes, they cry out, "But I work!" There are arguments on completing household chores because relatives stuck on their concepts of gender roles and duties will not take the time or make the effort to help one another.

How shameful it is for us to cry out to God for help while refusing to help those in our households. Are we seeking to serve or to be served?

We can maintain order and harmony within our households by practicing the teachings of the humble servant Jesus. His words have Lordship in our homes.

> But whosoever will be great among you, let him be your minister; And whosoever will be chief among you, let him be your servant: Even as the Son of man came not to be ministered unto, but to minister, and to give his life a ransom for many (Matt. 20:26–28).

> "For whether is greater, he that sitteth at meat, or he that serveth? is not he that sitteth at meat? but I am among you as he that serveth" (Luke 22:27).

Many families are struggling to stay connected, as communication has become rough, rushed, or rare. There are more expressed frustrations about household and financial issues, than impartations of encouragement, tenderness, patience, and humility. Some of us have become verbal strangers to those in our households.

In public, our family members hear strange sounds of patience, calm, and kindness coming out of our mouths. Our families look at us as if to say, "Who are you, and why don't we hear this at home?" At the other extreme, several of us barely speak at home, but we're the life of the conversation party in public or when interacting with nonfamily members.

Just as we must live the Christian life honestly, we cannot have hypocritical speech patterns.

Some of us are quick to say "Please" and Thank you" to strangers, bosses, and church leaders, while the people we live with rarely hear those words from us. In some households, such verbal kindness has been unheard of for years!

We cannot be spouses and parents who are verbally nice to other people and children, while engaging in rude, impatient, and insulting speech behaviors at home. Ungodly and unwise speaking at home—especially between spouses—negatively affects communication with the Lord.

> *Likewise, ye husbands, dwell with them according to knowledge, giving honour unto the wife, as unto the weaker vessel, and as being heirs together of the grace of life; that your prayers be not hindered* (1 Peter 3:7).

God says "the weaker vessel" is valuable and delicate and must be treated with respect and godly care so that the couple can enjoy "the grace of life"—His favor—together.

"That your prayers be not hindered" lets us know communication with the Lord—and its favorable results—can be blocked when wisdom is not used or respect is not given to those whom God declares valuable. Some people have exhibited merit-worthy efforts and qualifications, but have not received wage raises, job promotions, or ministry opportunities. They have yet to realize that their offensive behaviors at home have separated them from experiencing the favor the Lord has for them.

> *For thou, Lord, wilt bless the righteous; with favour wilt thou compass him as with a shield* (Ps. 5:12).

> *A good man obtaineth favour of the Lord: but a man of wicked devices will he condemn* (Prov. 12:2).

> *Behold, the Lord's hand is not shortened, that it cannot save; neither his ear heavy, that it cannot hear: But your iniquities have separated between you and your God, and your sins have hid his face from you, that he will not hear* (Isa. 59:1–2).

We must honestly allow the Lord to show us the answers to this question: Are we dishonoring those whom God has instructed us to value, while expecting Him to honor our prayer requests? While we do battle with satanic forces assigned to keep us from being blessed, we just cannot blame some things on the devil.

Our mouths can hold up the blessing process and progress of our marriages and households. This is not a gender issue, but a spiritual situation. What we believe in our hearts about verbal interactions at home will come out of our mouths.

> *Not that which goeth into the mouth defileth a man; but that which cometh out of the mouth, this defileth a man … But those things which proceed out of the mouth come forth from the heart; and they defile the man* (Matt. 15:11, 18).

> *A good man out of the good treasure of his heart bringeth forth that which is good; and an evil man out of the evil treasure of his heart bringeth forth that which is evil: for of the abundance of the heart his mouth speaketh* (Luke 6:45).

Sadly, a few of us do not believe we need to say "Please," "Thank you," "I love you," or "I appreciate you" at home. We ask, "Why say 'Thank you' to children for doing what they are supposed to do?" However, we are quick to allow insensitive words to freely flow from our hearts through our mouths and into the ears and hearts of our loved ones. Once spoken, what is in our hearts has settled in their hearts. A wounding cycle begins as hurtful words begin to flow from their hearts back to our hearts. This leads to verbal misconduct referred to as "railing for railing"—or insult for insult—as outlined in 1Peter 3:9.

God's word instructs us to have our minds, hearts, and tongues in right spiritual order as we speak with one another:

> *Finally, be ye all of one mind, having compassion one of another, love as brethren, be pitiful, be courteous: Not rendering evil for evil, or railing for railing: but contrariwise blessing; knowing that ye are thereunto called, that ye should inherit a blessing. For he that will love life, and see good days, let him refrain his tongue from evil, and his lips*

that they speak no guile: Let him eschew evil, and do good;
let him seek peace, and ensue it (1 Peter 3:8–11).

There are people living on pins and needles because they live with verbal volcanoes—spouses, parents, and children who are constantly erupting or seething their way to eruption.

We are instructed that getting angry does not give us the right to sin or hold grudges (Eph. 4:26). We are still responsible for our words and actions.

In James 1:20, we are taught that functioning in wrath—constant and uncontrolled anger, frustration, and rage—removes us from being in right standing with God. James 1:19 tells us how we ought to be, and this goes for behavior inside the home:

Wherefore, my beloved brethren, let every man be swift to
hear, slow to speak, slow to wrath.

Consider these wise words:

He that is slow to anger is better than the mighty; and
he that ruleth his spirit than he that taketh a city (Prov.
16:32).

More powerful than wrath is a soft answer, according to Proverbs 15:1. While harsh words stir up anger, a soft answer has the power to avert wrath.

A soft answer is not something we whisper or say in fear. A soft answer is a response given with the right words, in the right tone, and at the right time to bring solution, healing, or wisdom to a situation. The soft answer patiently works its way to the root of the issue without hurting or attacking others involved.

This powerful soft answer only comes from the Lord and can penetrate the hardest and harshest surfaces of the hearts, minds, and lives of those within our households.

The preparations of the heart in man, and the answer of
the tongue, is from the Lord (Prov. 16:1).

By long forbearing is a prince persuaded, and a soft tongue
breaketh the bone (Prov. 25:15).

Oftentimes, we must confront unpleasant issues and disagreeable behaviors in the household.

Many of us must be honest in admitting that when we are the correctors, we may not be understanding, patient, or fair about our assessments of the situations. Our comments may be critical, accusatory, or cold. Sometimes our attitude is this: "You're wrong, and you're going to pay the price."

However, we are quite different when it's our turn to be confronted or corrected. We can be argumentative, defensive, dismissive, or reluctant to recognize our faults and the problems they generate within the household.

The Lord has given us instructions in Galatians 6:1–3 to help our households overcome these issues:

> Brethren, if a man be overtaken in a fault, ye which are spiritual, restore such an one in the spirit of meekness; considering thyself, lest thou also be tempted. Bear ye one another's burdens, and so fulfil the law of Christ. For if a man think himself to be something, when he is nothing, he deceiveth himself.

We should address issues fully aware that we, too, are prone to making wrong decisions or engaging in habitual behaviors that bother or hurt our relatives.

"Ye which are spiritual" means those who practice addressing issues in accordance to the Word and will of God. Those "which are spiritual" also follow the leading of God's Spirit and behave according to the fruit of the Spirit outlined in Galatians 5:22–23.

Even in our households, the Lord can give us the words and show us the timing and balance for chastisements, corrections, and comfort.

As a Father to His people, the Lord sent prophets to announce punishments for sin and unrepentant attitudes. However, He knew when and how to send forgiving and restorative words to those He punished.

> And in that day thou shalt say, "O Lord, I will praise thee: though thou wast angry with me, thine anger is turned away, and thou comfortedst me" (Isa. 12:1).

> *"Comfort ye, comfort ye my people," saith your God. "Speak ye comfortably to Jerusalem, and cry unto her, that her warfare is accomplished, that her iniquity is pardoned: for she hath received of the Lord's hand double for all her sins"* (Isa. 40:1–2).

There also is a connection between the kingdom of God and our households. Submission to Christ and His ways is required of each spouse, parent, and child in recognition of the ultimate headship of God.

> *But I would have you know, that the head of every man is Christ; and the head of the woman is the man; and the head of Christ is God* (1 Cor. 11:3).

> *Wives, submit yourselves unto your own husbands, as unto the Lord ... Husbands, love your wives, even as Christ also loved the church, and gave himself for it ... So ought men to love their wives as their own bodies. He that loveth his wife loveth himself ... Nevertheless let every one of you in particular so love his wife even as himself; and the wife see that she reverence her husband* (Eph. 5:22, 25, 28, 33).

> *Wives, submit yourselves unto your own husbands, as it is fit in the Lord. Husbands, love your wives, and be not bitter against them. Children, obey your parents in all things: for this is well pleasing unto the Lord. Fathers, provoke not your children to anger, lest they be discouraged* (Col. 3:18–21).

Note the words "bitter," "against," "provoke," "anger," and "discouraged" in Colossians 3:18–21. Do any of these words describe the atmosphere and verbal behaviors in our households?

Receive the word of the Lord as He shows us our homework assignment for our hearts and mouths.

> *Let all bitterness, and wrath, and anger, and clamour, and evil speaking, be put away from you, with all malice: And be ye kind one to another, tenderhearted, forgiving one*

another, even as God for Christ's sake hath forgiven you
(Eph. 4:31–32).

Now, review Colossians 3:18–21 and note the words "submit," "love," "obey," and "pleasing." Have we matured in these four areas in our relationship with the Lord? Does this maturity show in our words and actions at home? Are we using any of these four words to excuse controlling, demanding, or self-absorbed behaviors at home?

Families can be healed, restored, revived, and transformed as they obey the instructions the Lord gives concerning these four words: submit, love, obey, and pleasing.

> *Submit yourselves therefore to God. Resist the devil, and he will flee from you* (James 4:7).

> *"And thou shalt love the Lord thy God with all thy heart, and with all thy soul, and with all thy mind, and with all thy strength: this is the first commandment. And the second is like, namely this, Thou shalt love thy neighbour as thyself. There is none other commandment greater than these"* (Mark 12:30–31).

> *Ye shall walk after the Lord your God, and fear him, and keep his commandments, and obey his voice, and ye shall serve him, and cleave unto him* (Deut. 13:4).

> *Then said Jesus unto them … "but as my Father hath taught me, I speak these things. And he that sent me is with me: the Father hath not left me alone; for I do always those things that please him"* (John 8:28, 29).

As Jesus demonstrated with His Father, we are to humble ourselves in the sight of the Lord (James 4:10) and under the mighty hand of God (1 Peter 5:6). Even in the home, we are not to esteem ourselves over one another. Doing so is the work of pride and of the flesh.

> *Let nothing be done through strife or vainglory; but in lowliness of mind let each esteem other better than themselves. Look not every man on his own things, but every man also on the things of others* (Phil. 2:3–4).

Another homework assignment is to be mindful of following the Lord's vocal cues.

Some people are spiritually tone-deaf to God's instructions on how they are to sound when they speak. They do not believe their voice tones cause problems.

Even the Lord is attentive in how He speaks to us. His voice is powerful and limitless. Yet He knows the right tone to use while addressing our situations and us. For example, while dealing with a discouraged and weary prophet Elijah, the Lord used a "still small voice" (1 Kings 19:12).

However, Joel 3:16 highlights a much different vocal characteristic of the Lord:

> *The Lord also shall roar out of Zion, and utter his voice from Jerusalem; and the heavens and the earth shall shake: but the Lord will be the hope of his people, and the strength of the children of Israel.*

In Isaiah 58:1, the Lord gave instructions on how to preach His words to His people:

> *"Cry aloud, spare not, lift up thy voice like a trumpet, and shew my people their transgression, and the house of Jacob their sins."*

The Lord also shows us the proper sounds to make at the appropriate times. For instance, the insurmountable walls surrounding the city of Jericho came down after the Israelites followed the marching and shouting orders given by God, as detailed in Joshua 6.

Israel was directed to "shout with a great shout" at a specific time. The people were to follow the shouting commands of Joshua, their leader. Sounds from a ram's horn and a trumpet were the people's signals that shouting time had come. Until then, the Israelites could not speak or make any vocal sounds whatsoever as they marched for days around Jericho.

> *And Joshua had commanded the people, saying, "Ye shall not shout, nor make any noise with your voice, neither shall any word proceed out of your mouth, until the day I bid you shout; then shall ye shout"* (Josh. 6:10).

The Lord had promised that Jericho's walls would fall after Israel completed its vocal obedience. Let us read the victorious results, knowing that the Lord has victory planned for us, as well:

> *And it came to pass at the seventh time, when the priests blew with the trumpets, Joshua said unto the people, "Shout; for the Lord hath given you the city" ... So the people shouted when the priests blew with the trumpets: and it came to pass, when the people heard the sound of the trumpet, and the people shouted with a great shout, that the wall fell down flat, so that the people went up into the city, every man straight before him, and they took the city"* (Josh. 6:16, 20).

Are we missing vocal cues concerning our homes? Have we obeyed the vocal assignments the Lord has given us for our families?

We must recognize there are some household walls that will only come down when we become verbally obedient to the Lord.

Let Us Pray

Lord, we humbly receive Your words, guidance, and touch as You instruct us to keep our mouths in godly order in our homes. Amen.

CHAPTER 12

Touched to Speak

During Jesus' time on earth, unbelieving religious leaders tried several times to arrest him.

In John 7:32–46, they sent officers to get Jesus, who was speaking to a crowd at the time. After hearing the Savior, the officers dared not arrest him, so they returned to their leaders empty-handed. The leaders demanded to know why the officers failed to make the arrest.

> *The officers answered, "Never man spake like this man"* (John 7:46).

There is no one who can speak like the Lord. He desires to speak through us in unique and powerful ways as He uses us to minister to others.

We have never spoken the way the Lord will touch our tongues to speak.

Before becoming a prophet, Isaiah had a remarkable tongue-touching experience with God. While receiving a vision of God's holiness and glory, Isaiah—convicted of his own transgressions—confessed the sinful condition of his life and lips.

> *Then said I, "Woe is me! For I am undone; because I am a man of unclean lips, and I dwell in the midst of a people of unclean lips: for mine eyes have seen the King, the Lord of hosts"* (Isa. 6:5).

Then one of God's angels took burning coal from the temple's altar.

> *And he laid it upon my mouth, and said, "Lo, this hath touched thy lips; and thine iniquity is taken away, and thy sin purged" (Isa. 6:7).*

After that, Isaiah committed to a prophetic life of obediently speaking God's words to His people. Never before had Isaiah spoken that way.

The same can be said of the prophet Jeremiah, who also had a tongue-touching experience with God.

In recalling his experience, the prophet begins by saying, "The word of the Lord came to me" (Jer. 1:4). Then in verse 5, Jeremiah recalled how the Lord informed him that his prophetic calling was determined before his birth. Jeremiah thought otherwise of himself and responded to the Lord accordingly.

> *Then said I, "Ah, Lord God! Behold, I cannot speak: for I am a child" (Jer. 1: 6).*

However, the Lord got the last word—and touch—concerning the issue:

> *Then the Lord put forth his hand, and touched my mouth. And the Lord said unto me, "Behold, I have put my words in thy mouth" (Jer. 1:9).*

Like other prophets, Jeremiah suffered for declaring the Lord's words. Repeatedly rejected, beaten, and imprisoned, Jeremiah decided he'd had enough of being God's prophet. However, the word of God proved to be too powerful for Jeremiah to hold.

> *Then I said, "I will not make mention of him, nor speak any more in his name." But his word was in mine heart as a burning fire shut up in my bones, and I was weary with forbearing, and I could not stay (Jer. 20:9).*

Through Jeremiah's experience, we learn that going through a tongue-touching experience with the Lord yields the obedience and results He wants from us in everything He calls us to say and do.

"But I don't know what to say" is the best thing to say to God. Of course, we don't know what to say. We have never spoken that way before. The Lord knows what we should say, how to say it, and who needs to hear it. Not depending on our words puts us in a perfect position to open ourselves to the Lord, allowing Him to touch our tongues and put His words in our mouths.

> *How sweet are thy words unto my taste! Yea, sweeter than honey to my mouth* (Ps. 119:103).

Mouths Open to His Words

> *I opened my mouth, and panted: for I longed for thy commandments* (Ps. 119:131).

Like Isaiah and Jeremiah, Ezekiel had a life-changing mouth moment with God during his call to be a prophet. In a vision, God presented Ezekiel a scroll filled with His words.

> *"Open thy mouth, and eat that I give thee" ... So I opened my mouth, and he caused me to eat that roll ... Then did I eat it; and it was in my mouth as honey for sweetness* (Ezek. 2:8 and 3:2, 3).

Afterward, God told Ezekiel what to do with the words imparted to him. The newly-appointed prophet was to first receive and hear God's words in his heart, then deliver them to the people (Ezek. 3:10–11). God restructured Ezekiel's life and speaking habits, revealing He had complete charge of Ezekiel's tongue.

> *"And I will make thy tongue cleave to the roof of thy mouth, that thou shalt be dumb ... But when I speak with thee, I will open thy mouth, and thou shalt say unto them, 'Thus saith the Lord God'"* (Ezek. 3:26, 27).

We also need a tongue-touching experience that prepares us for the impartation of the Lord's will, words, tone, and timing.

"Ephphatha" ... "Be Opened": Hearing What to Speak

The tongue-touching experience with the Lord includes an intimate process in which He corrects our speech by healing our hearing problems. Jesus demonstrated this with a man who was deaf and had a speech impediment, as detailed in Mark 7:31–35.

Jesus pulled the man away from the crowd. Though the public knew about the man's issues, his healing moment with Jesus was a private matter. Jesus began the intimate healing process by putting His fingers into the man's ear. He then developed an even deeper connection with the man's tongue.

> *And he spit, and touched his tongue, and looking up to heaven, he sighed, and saith unto him, "Ephphatha," that is, "Be opened." And straightway his ears were opened, and the string of his tongue was loosed, and he spake plain* (Mark 7:33–35).

In using His saliva, Jesus—the Word who became flesh (John 1:14)—anointed the man's tongue, destroying the yoke that stalled the man's speech. Jesus first dealt with the man's ears because the hearing disability negatively affected speech capabilities. The man could not audibly determine how to form words or make proper sounds, leading to the development of a speech impediment.

Some of us have similar issues spiritually. We have not taken into account how much hearing and speaking capabilities are interconnected. Thus, we struggle to communicate effectively with people. We are unable to develop honest, positive, upright, and wise speaking habits. Our speech lacks godly direction.

We cannot hear the Lord's Spirit, so we do not speak according to the things of the Spirit. We can't hear peace, so we don't speak peace. We can't hear kindness and patience, so we don't speak kindness and patience. We can't hear healing, so we don't speak healing. We can't hear grace, so we don't speak with grace.

Some of us want to speak in God-pleasing ways, but do not know how because we never heard these ways while growing up. However, a few of us simply refuse to hear instruction on how to speak humbly and with the grace of God. Like the man who received healing, we can let Jesus change our lives by giving him intimate access to our ears and mouths.

The Lord can speak, "Ephphatha, be opened" to our ears. Then those closed areas within us will open to Him. He can bring us through the obstacles that keep us from hearing Him. He will anoint our tongues, loosening them to speak the right ways, as we acknowledge Him as the Lord of our tongues and Master of our mouths.

> *Hear; for I will speak of excellent things; and the opening of my lips shall be right things* (Prov. 8:6).

> *"What I tell you in darkness, that speak ye in light: and what ye hear in the ear, that preach ye upon the housetops"* (Matt. 10:27).

CHAPTER 13

Instructions for Speaking to the Weary

The Lord GOD hath given me the tongue of the learned, that I should know how to speak a word in season to him that is weary: he wakeneth morning by morning, he wakeneth mine ear to hear as the learned (Isa. 50:4).

The Lord is a companion to those who are weary. Weary people do not need to hear our thoughts, opinions, or advice. They need words that flow from the Lord's heart to their lives. Our humanly limited tongues are unable to deliver those words, but the Lord can give us a tongue that can.

We receive this tongue by crying out to the Lord, "Not my words, but Your words be said and done." We must humbly ask the Lord for His words of wisdom for every weary situation.

If any of you lack wisdom, let him ask of God, that giveth to all men liberally, and upbraideth not; and it shall be given him (James 1:5).

The Lord will begin to deal with us about words, phrases, and Scriptures to share. He will direct our voice tones and body language. He also will instruct us on the times and places to speak.

The tongue of the learned is a tongue instructed, disciplined, and corrected to be obedient, wise, and well-versed in how to deliver the Lord's words according to His will. The learned tongue knows how to speak to people who are exhausted by the challenges of life, because this tongue also knows the words of those who feel crushed, defeated, empty, useless, used up, unwanted, and washed out.

> *I am weary with my groaning; all the night make I my bed to swim; I water my couch with my tears* (Ps. 6:6).

> *I am poured out like water, and all my bones are out of joint: my heart is like wax; it is melted in the midst of my bowels* (Ps. 22:14).

> *My tears have been my meat day and night, while they continually say unto me, "Where is thy God?"* (Ps. 42:3).

> *I looked on my right hand, and beheld, but there was no man that would know me: refuge failed me; no man cared for my soul ... Attend unto my cry; for I am brought very low ... Bring my soul out of prison, that I may praise thy name ...* (Ps. 142:4, 6, 7).

The pain is great, and the weariness is deep. However, God has words to lead every soul through the darkness to find salvation, deliverance, and a refreshing experience in Him.

> *Thy word is a lamp to my feet and a light unto my path* (Ps. 119:105).

> *Cause me to hear thy lovingkindness in the morning; for in thee do I trust: cause me to know the way wherein I should walk; for I lift my soul unto thee* (Ps. 143:8).

This is why we should pray that His words touch our tongues and fill our mouths. We must be equipped spiritually and verbally to serve and strengthen the weary. Then we are not going to the weary with a tongue full of pep talk and catch phrases, but with the Lord's anointed words capable of destroying yokes of weariness off their lives.

> *Strengthen ye the weak hands, and confirm the feeble knees. Say to them that are of a fearful heart, "Be strong, fear not: behold, your God will come with vengeance, even God with a recompence; he will come and save you"* (Isa. 35:3–4).

The Lord is patient, kind, understanding, forgiving, full of compassion, and full of love. He knows how to embrace and heal weary souls.

"For I have satiated the weary soul, and I have replenished every sorrowful soul" (Jer. 31:25).

From Bitter to Blessed

The Lord replenished Naomi, an Israelite woman who lost her husband and their two sons several years after their move to a foreign country, as told in Ruth 1. Having suffered such losses, a weary Naomi decided to return to her hometown of Bethlehem.

As she prepared for a lonely and mournful journey, Naomi told her two daughters-in-law, Orpah and Ruth, to return to their mothers' home. Orpah returned home, but Ruth held onto Naomi, insisting on going to Bethlehem. Ruth passionately spoke to Naomi with words of companionship, faithfulness, and commitment.

And Ruth said, "Intreat me not to leave thee, or to return from following after thee: for whither thou goest, I will go; and where thou lodgest, I will lodge: thy people shall be my people, and thy God my God: where thou diest, will I die, and there will I be buried: the Lord do so to me, and more also, if ought but death part thee and me" (Ruth 1:16–17).

Naomi finally accepted Ruth's companionship. The journey experience resulted in a great blessing for both women. However, the wonderful ending took time.

First, Naomi and Ruth had to travel from Moab to Bethlehem. When they finally reached their destination, Naomi was less than happy during her homecoming conversation with the Bethlehem women.

And she said unto them, "Call me not Naomi, call me Mara: for the Almighty hath dealt very bitterly with me. I went out full, and the Lord hath brought me home again empty: why then call ye me Naomi, seeing the Lord hath testified against me, and the Almighty hath afflicted me?" (Ruth 1:20–21).

However, God was with Naomi through Ruth's companionship. He enabled Ruth to work in the fields to provide food for Naomi. Ruth's presence also kept a childless Naomi functioning as a mother and woman of wisdom.

Through Naomi's instructions, the Lord blessed Ruth with a new marriage and a child. After the birth of Obed—Ruth and Boaz's son—the Bethlehem women celebrated the replenishing of Naomi's family and future.

> *And the women said unto Naomi, "Blessed be the Lord, which hath not left thee this day without a kinsman, that his name may be famous in Israel. And he shall be unto thee a restorer of thy life, and a nourisher of thine old age: for thy daughter in law, which loveth thee, which is better to thee than seven sons, hath born him." And Naomi took the child, and laid it in her bosom, and became nurse unto it*" (Ruth 4:14–16).

At the start of her new life's journey, a weary and grief-stricken Naomi called herself "bitter." However, the Lord confirmed through the townswomen that He was with Naomi all along to bless her. The Lord had moved through Ruth to clutch onto Naomi, who wanted to journey alone. He inspired Ruth to speak the words that got hold of Naomi's heart and started the two women on a journey that would become biblical history.

A Compassionate, Committed Companion to the Weary

Ruth's relationship with Naomi shows us how God intimately connects with us, especially in our weary times.

> *In the day when I cried thou answeredst me, and strengthenedst me with strength in my soul* (Ps. 138:3).

> *"Peace I leave with you, my peace I give unto you … Let not your heart be troubled, neither let it be afraid"* (John 14:27).

> *"I am with you always, even unto the end of the world"* (Matt. 28:20).

"I will never leave thee, nor forsake thee" (Heb. 13:5).

Those who are weary need words of compassion, companionship, and commitment. They must be reassured that someone will stick with them, especially during the times when they speak of their bitterness, emptiness, and grief.

Sometimes they are discouraged from honestly expressing their thoughts and emotions. Well-meaning people tell them not to say "those things" or not to "feel that way." Yet the Lord hears them, and He has loving, comforting, and reassuring words concerning where they are in their experiences mentally, emotionally, and spiritually.

The Lord gives words that stick with the weary as Ruth stuck with Naomi. His word will work on the weary ones' behalf and bring in harvests of good things as Ruth did for Naomi. The Lord has words that will move the weary from the bitter to the blessed places of life as we saw with these two women.

Like Naomi, there are people who insist on telling us to go the other way as they prepare to deal with their hurts alone. Some of them are long-distant loved ones. However, the Lord can show us what words to speak or send to them in letters and cards. While we may not be around them physically, we have faith that God's words will be their companion.

Like Ruth, we must be willing to make sacrifices so the Lord can use us to revive weary souls. Ruth gave up her family and hometown to serve Naomi and Naomi's God. While we may not have to literally move to minister to the weary, our mouths will have to go through a moving process. Some of us have family or hometown communication styles we must leave behind as the Lord releases unto us the tongue of the learned.

Oftentimes, our speaking habits toward people in weary situations can get in the way of how the Lord desires to express Himself. He knows the root of their weariness, while we only speak to the symptoms we see. For instance, there are people who go from job to job or can only keep jobs for short periods. On the surface, they may be viewed as lazy or not having the stick-to-it attitude. However, the real issue is they have difficulty in the work environment because the idea of dealing with bosses and coworkers exhausts them. For most of their lives, they have witnessed unresolved conflicts at home, school, church, and family gatherings.

They were not taught successful problem-solving skills while growing up. Weary from lives filled with constant tension, they go from job to job—or relationship to relationship—looking for peaceful and emotionally safe environments where they can function.

On top of all that, these weary ones are getting lectures about work ethics, not knowing the Lord has life-changing words for them.

The Lord can use us to talk to them about His healing peace that has the power to mend the wounds of their past, to encourage them to seek His answers for conflict resolution, and to show them how to remain tranquil in tense situations.

Some of us get impatient with—and even insulted by—other people's struggles. Thus, we make comments like: "I got through it; so can you." "You're not the only one having hard times, so you need to get it together." "There are other people who had it worse than you, and they turned out just fine."

Speakers of these words have put their frustrations and verbal and emotional needs ahead of their weary listeners. These words only serve to make the speakers feel better.

We cannot forget that though we may have similar experiences, God still relates to everyone individually and intimately. The God-given tongue of the learned understands this truth and behaves accordingly.

There are people so verbally proud and full of themselves, they mouth their way into weary people's situations. They think their suggestions, prayers, and spiritual lectures will make the difference, solve the problem, or get people moving in the right direction. Then they stand there, relishing in their verbal heroics with their proud tongues waving in the wind like superhero capes. Yet the weary are left without refreshing words that will turn their lives around.

Consider Job's experience. He and his wife endured the deaths of their children, servants, and herdsmen, and the loss of their livestock (Job 1). Then Job suffered long-term and severe health issues, as "sore boils" covered him from head to toe (Job 2:7).

Job's grieving wife told him to curse God and die (Job 2:9), and his three friends—Eliphaz, Bildad, and Zophar—insisted his suffering was a result of some awful sin he must have committed. They advised him to confess and repent. The friends initially mourned with Job and comforted him. However, as Job continued to suffer, they supported him less and accused him more.

Job desperately yearned for God's words.

> *I would order my cause before him, and fill my mouth with arguments. I would know the words which he would answer, and understand what he would say unto me. Will he plead against me with his great power? No; but he would put strength in me ... Neither have I gone back from the commandment of his lips; I have esteemed the words of his mouth more than my necessary food* (Job 23:4–6, 12).

Though Job suffered awhile, the Lord restored him. He gave Job more children and doubled the possessions Job had prior to his horrific experiences.

The Lord also had some words for Job's friends.

> *The Lord spoke to Eliphaz the Temanite, "My wrath is kindled against thee, and against thy two friends: for ye have not spoken of me the thing that is right, as my servant Job hath"* (Job 42:7).

Their words added weariness to Job's woes. This is why we need the Lord to give us the tongue of the learned. It will keep us from making verbal errors that wound the weary.

When People Cause Their Own Weariness

There will be times the Lord will call us to patiently minister to people who cause their own weary conditions. No matter how many times we have given them warnings or offered wise counsel, they have insisted on going in directions leading to troublesome episodes. We cannot gloat when they learn the hard way that our counsel was correct.

In Proverbs 24:17–18, we are instructed not to gloat over the defeat of our enemies. How much more should we not engage in such behavior or attitudes toward our families, coworkers, or fellow church members when they admit their errors?

We should avoid comments like "I told you so," or "See, I was right," or "They should have listened to me." In making such comments, we are setting ourselves up to be praised, rather than giving God the glory for revealing the wisdom needed for keeping our lives, households, and ministries on the right paths. Remember, we are not above being right one minute and wrong the next second.

We must maintain the right attitude while dealing with the weary, especially when the consequences of their actions trap us, causing us weariness. In Acts 27, we see that the apostle Paul endured a similar situation and had to minister in the midst of extreme trouble and weariness. We can learn from his interaction with sailors who initially refused his wise counsel, putting passengers' lives at risk.

Paul was among a group of prisoners on a ship sailing to Rome when a dangerous wind challenged the vessel. The apostle warned that the ship's cargo could be lost and passengers' lives endangered if the crew continued with their travel plans. The crew ignored his warning and continued sailing. They came upon an even harsher wind that violently tossed the ship. Going without food, the crew and passengers worked hard to keep the vessel afloat, even throwing cargo overboard. Nothing worked. They soon lost hope that everyone's lives would be saved.

Paul then spoke to the crew again.

> *"Sirs, ye should have hearkened unto me, and not have loosed from Crete, and to have gained this harm and loss"*
> (Acts 27:21).

Please understand that the apostle was not gloating. His words do not give us permission or an excuse to adopt an "I told you so" attitude in speech.

Paul was a prisoner among unbelievers. He was reminding them of his earlier counsel in efforts to confirm his credibility as God's spokesperson during an ongoing life-and-death crisis. The apostle was about to deliver another life-sustaining word from God. The crew and passengers needed to listen in order to survive. Paul did not make himself the focus as he revealed the source of the words he was saying:

> *"And now I exhort you to be of good cheer: for there shall be no loss of any man's life among you, but of the ship. For there stood by me this night the angel of God, whose I am*

and whom I serve, saying, 'Fear not, Paul; thou must be brought before Caesar: and lo, God hath given thee all them that sail with thee.' Wherefore, sirs, be of good cheer: for I believe God, that it shall be even as it was told me" (Acts 27:22–25).

The crisis at sea continued after Paul spoke, but the crew and passengers—including soldiers who had charge of the prisoners—had a life promise from God.

Yet, the crew secretly tried to escape on a small boat they lowered to the sea under the guise of casting anchors. However, Paul told the soldiers about the crew's plans. He reminded the soldiers that everyone had to stay on the ship to preserve their lives. The soldiers cut the small boat's ties to the ship, letting it float away.

The weary travelers also heeded Paul's counsel to eat, as they had gone fourteen days without food while trying to keep the ship afloat. The apostle took some bread, thanked God for it, and began to eat.

Then were they all of good cheer, and they also took some meat (Acts 27:36).

Their crisis continued as overpowering waves forced the ship to run aground, breaking apart the vessel in the sea. In the midst of the chaos, the soldiers decided to kill all the prisoners to keep them from escaping. Their commander stopped them because he wanted to save Paul.

Everyone either swam or used parts of the ship to get to shore. Everything happened according to God's guarantee that the ship would be lost, but their lives saved.

The apostle Paul was able to minister to the weary people around him because he remained focused on God's words. He showed everyone how to receive, believe, speak, and cleave to God's words while being tossed about in wearying circumstances. In fact, he twice encouraged the despondent and worn-out crew to "Be of good cheer" (Acts 27:22–25) even though they were the ones who put themselves and others in the dangerous situation.

Oftentimes, some of us want to see the opposite of "good cheer" for people who made wrong decisions that caused themselves and others to suffer. We may want to watch them suffer, mope around, or drown in the sea of problems and weariness they created. "They made their bed; now let them lie in it," we may think, or even dare to say.

In Paul's situation, the ship's crew suffered the consequences of their decisions. They lost cargo, and their bodies underwent distress as they worked vigorously to save the ship. However, the Lord, Whose mercy endures forever, inspired Paul to urge everyone to "Be of good cheer."

There are weary people around us who need to hear these words today. They need to know that God loves them and is here to save them from their self-generated troubles.

Can God trust us to abandon our tirades and accept His instructions on how to speak to them? Can He use us to deliver to them messages of "good cheer"—of hope, encouragement, and assuredness of His presence, forgiveness, and deliverance?

There are many times in the Bible where God spoke comfort to His weary people while they were living through the consequences of their sins. The Lord sent his prophets, including Isaiah, to speak comforting and merciful words to His people.

> *And in that day thou shalt say, "O Lord, I will praise thee: though thou wast angry with me, thine anger is turned away, and thou comfortedst me"* (Isa. 12:1).

> *"Comfort ye, comfort ye my people," saith your God. "Speak comfortably to Jerusalem, and cry unto her, that her warfare is accomplished, that her iniquity is pardoned: for she hath received of the Lord's hand double for all her sins"* (Isa. 40:1–2).

> *"In a little wrath I hid my face from thee for a moment; but with everlasting kindness will I have mercy on thee," saith the Lord thy Redeemer* (Isa. 54:8).

When We Are the Weary Ones Who Are Wrong

Some of us are the weary wrong ones who need God to deliver us from the consequences of our words and actions. However, we often do not speak such sentiments on behalf of others when we become weary of their wrongdoings. In other words, we want judgment for them, but mercy for ourselves. We are overlooking the fact that the Lord is willing to save *all* who repent.

*For thou, Lord, art good, and ready to forgive; and plenteous
in mercy unto all them that call upon thee* (Ps. 86:5).

*The Lord is gracious, and full of compassion; slow to anger,
and of great mercy* (Ps. 145:8).

Let us learn from the experience of the prophet Jonah, who caused his own weary situation when he initially disobeyed God's command to preach salvation to Nineveh, a wicked city. Jonah was apprehensive about going to Nineveh because of its history of brutality against Israel and other nations. The prophet wanted God to judge it, not save it. This evil country certainly did not deserve God's mercy, the prophet figured. Therefore, Jonah tried to run—or rather, sail—away from his assignment.

Instead, the prophet found himself in some weary situations. He was thrown off a ship and then swallowed by a great fish, remaining in its belly for three days.

Jonah had enough. He cried out to God, vowing to do His will.

The Lord released Jonah from the fish's belly and put him on the road to Nineveh.

The prophet then preached God's words of salvation, which the people immediately accepted. They repented of their sins, and God spared their lives.

But Jonah again put himself in a weary situation. After his preaching, Jonah set up a booth outside Nineveh, waiting to see what became of the city (Jonah 4:5). When Nineveh received God's mercy, the prophet was angry.

To deal with Jonah's wrong attitude, the Lord allowed a plant to grow and provide a refreshing shadow for the prophet. The next day, the Lord allowed the plant to die, while intensifying the sun's heat on the prophet. Jonah suffered so much, he became angry about the situation and wished for his own death.

God used this experience to confront a weary Jonah about having more compassion for one plant than for the more than 120,000 souls God wanted to save and lead in His righteousness.

*"And should not I spare Nineveh, that great city, wherein
are more than sixscore thousand persons that cannot discern*

between their right hand and their left hand; and also much cattle?" (Jonah 4:11).

Are we in weary situations because of our wrong attitudes, behaviors, and decisions? We can overcome these wearisome ways by turning to our righteous Lord who knows the directions for our lives. Let us be eager to go His way as He makes plain His will and His paths.

A Savior to the Weary

For when we were yet without strength, in due time Christ died for the ungodly. For scarcely for a righteous man will one die: yet peradventure for a good man some would even dare to die. But God commendeth his love toward us, in that, while we were yet sinners, Christ died for us (Rom. 5:6–8).

A thief was dying on a cross, the penalty for his wrongdoing. On another cross near him was Jesus. Hanging on a third cross was a second thief, who chided Jesus, demanding that Jesus get all of them out of their cross crises. The first thief rebuked the second thief, stating that Jesus was innocent, while they were guilty and deserved to die.

The remorseful first thief turned his attention to Jesus. What came next was a brief, but extraordinary, conversation between a weary sinner and the weary Savior.

And he said unto Jesus, "Lord, remember me when thou comest into thy kingdom." And Jesus said unto him, "Verily I say unto thee, Today shalt thou be with me in paradise" (Luke 23:42–43).

The weary, remorseful thief still had to face his earthly death-penalty consequences, but he had repented, received forgiveness, and would spend eternity with Jesus.

While dying for sins He did not commit, Jesus still had the power to save a thief—and us—while we were yet sinners with no ability to save ourselves. Even in His own time of cross weariness, Jesus was kind, forgiving, loving, merciful, and sensitive to the weary soul. He truly paid the price for us to speak refreshingly to the weary.

CHAPTER 14

Instructions for Forgiving Our Tongues

Let us be honest: some of us have communication styles capable of making the weary wearier. Many of us are guilty of sinning against God and wounding others with our tongues. We did not intend to err verbally, but we did.

Having read the last three chapters about the Lord's instructions regarding our tongues, several of us are now realizing how verbally insensitive we have been. We also are recognizing that some of our troublesome situations stem from us reaping the results of harsh words we have sown through criticizing, gossiping, judging, hollering, and name-calling. We have even gone so far as to humiliate in public relatives, friends, and strangers.

As we move into the forgiveness portion of our tongue instructions, we yet have more verbal issues we need to acknowledge, as we need to change our mouth behaviors as signs of true repentance.

God holds us responsible for how we speak to others. They, too, are His creations, and He wants nothing He created to be verbally disrespected, mistreated, or wounded. Disrespect for the Lord is at the root of ungodly verbal behaviors and word choices.

Though the Lord created our tongues to serve and please Him, some of us seem to have our own mission statement about our mouths: "It's my mouth, and I'll say what I want to say, when I want to say it, where I want to say it, how I want to say it, and to whomever I want to say it."

Many people think they are in control of their tongues, but the Lord reveals otherwise:

> *But the tongue can no man tame; it is an unruly evil, full of deadly poison. Therewith bless we God, even the Father; and therewith curse we men, which are made after the similitude of God. Out of the same mouth proceedeth blessing and cursing. My brethren, these things ought not so to be* (James 3:8–10).

Cursing does not necessarily mean the use of those certain four- and five-letter words, but the use of abusive or injurious words and voice tones that cause the hearers to feel they are devalued. No blessings come from speaking habits that demean others.

Several of us say or think, "If they don't want to hear it, they can go somewhere else. I don't care." This ungodly and dangerous mind-set ensures we will continue hurting the people we have already wounded.

When we don't care, we won't hear the painful question the hearers are really asking us:

> *"How long will ye vex my soul, and break me in pieces with words?"* (Job 19:2).

Some of us are guilty of verbally tearing down relatives, friends, coworkers, and fellow congregants because of our win-at-all-costs attitude while confronting issues. The verbal exchanges we help generate get so heated, we move from working to resolve matters to attacking our counterparts with words. We just have to win.

Some of us like to say our piece and then walk away while other people are yet responding. At the other extreme are people all in for the verbal long haul, standing toe-to-toe and nose to nose with their counterparts, determined to have the last say.

While some people yell, others calmly speak calculated words, with the motive of getting the upper hand on those with whom they are speaking. This seemingly calm verbal approach is not fooling God.

The words of his mouth were smoother than butter, but war was in his heart: his words were softer than oil, yet were they drawn swords (Ps. 55:21).

The Lord is putting a mirror in front of our mouths to help us recognize our unacceptable verbal behaviors and their effect on Him, others, and ourselves. Some of us will not take our tongues to the Lord in repentance because we refuse to acknowledge that we have verbal issues that need correction. However, the Lord desires that we all turn to Him with humility and repentance as we ask Him to forgive our tongue transgressions.

Let us have a "Selah" moment as we pause to reflect on the encouraging and restorative words of Psalm 32:1–2 and 5:

Blessed is he whose transgression is forgiven, whose sin is covered. Blessed is the man unto whom the Lord imputeth not iniquity, and in whose spirit there is no guile ... I acknowledged my sin unto thee, and mine iniquity have I not hid. I said, "I will confess my transgressions unto the Lord"; and thou forgavest the iniquity of my sin. Selah.

While confessing our tongue transgressions, we cannot forget to pray for those we have hurt with our words. We ask the Lord to heal their wounds and to help them forgive us. We also seek the Lord's guidance on how to go to them with humility and apology.

Some of us may have to send letters or cards or make phone calls. The idea is not to explain ourselves, but to acknowledge that we hurt them and to say, "I'm sorry. Please forgive me."

In some cases, people will not accept our apologies. They will insist that we do not deserve forgiveness. While we are honestly remorseful for our verbal wrongs, we cannot allow a spirit of condemnation to oppress or torment us with guilt, shame, frustration, and heaviness. We must trust in the Lord's forgiveness and continue our fellowship with Him, while keeping the people we offended in loving prayer. The Lord cares for everyone involved in these situations and extends His healing touch to those who will receive Him.

Several of us are troubled because we want to express our apologies to certain individuals, but cannot because we have lost contact with them due to severed relationships, their unknown locations, or deaths.

Hence, memories of our errors have trapped our minds, keeping us from moving forward mentally, spiritually, and emotionally. Our hearts ache because those issues seem to have no resolution. However, we have forgotten that we do have a solution.

We can take our confessions and feelings to the Lord and reread the liberating words of Psalm 32:1, 2, and 5.

Have faith that the Lord will continue His work of leading us to spiritual—and verbal—success.

> *"I will instruct thee and teach thee in the way which thou shalt go: I will guide thee with mine eye" (Ps. 32:8).*

We must allow His words to free our minds and hearts. The Lord can move us past our feelings and into the knowledge that He truly has forgiven us. Then we can thank the Lord for putting us—and our mouths—in right standing with Him.

Now, let us read Psalm 32:11 and receive the blessing of joy that comes with God's forgiveness:

> *Be glad in the Lord, and rejoice, ye righteous: and shout for joy, all ye that are upright in heart.*

When Jesus died on the cross for our sins, this included our tongue transgressions. He cleared the way for our forgiveness and for our mouths to be in right relationship with God. The Lord's forgiveness brings relief as He mercifully replaces hurts with healings. The door is open for us to renew our commitment to allow the Lord to use our mouths to spread the gospel, testify of His greatness, and verbally bless people in our homes, churches, and communities.

Jesus is our ultimate example of how to maintain righteous verbal behavior. During his time on earth, Jesus taught that he did not speak self-generated words, but those imparted by God, His Father.

> *"I do nothing of myself; but as my father hath taught me, I speak these things ... For I have spoken not of myself; but the Father which sent me, he gave me a commandment, what I should say, and what I should speak. And I know that his commandment is life everlasting: whatsoever I speak therefore, even as the Father said unto me, so I speak"* (John 8:28 and 12:49–50).

CHAPTER 15

Instructions for Instructors
Part I: Accepting Rejection

Rejection, scorn, ignored teachings, disobedient hearers—such are the trials of instructors sent by God.

For instructors, there are the powerful experiences of receiving teachings and wisdom from the Lord through the Holy Spirit. We treasure the Lord's thoughts, and we worship Him as He relates to us in unique and transformative ways. While there are revelations He commissions us to share, there are people who are not willing to receive them.

Hurt, loneliness, and anger can develop within us if we do not allow our Great Instructor to strengthen and heal us from these rejection circumstances.

Throughout the Bible are details of how people rejected, disobeyed, and ignored the Lord and His words.

In Jeremiah 23:33–40, people asked the prophet several times, "What is the burden of the Lord?" as though the Lord's messages were bothersome interruptions to their lives.

Before beginning prophetic ministry in Israel, Ezekiel was told his work and words would not be accepted because people had become "impudent and hardhearted" (Ezek. 3:7).

Our saving teacher, Jesus, warned His disciples that rejection would be part of their ministry experience.

"If ye were of the world, the world would love his own: but because ye are not of the world, but I have chosen you out of the world, therefore the world hateth you ... If they have persecuted me, they will also persecute you" (John 15:19, 20).

The Lord forewarns us of hard-hearted responses so we will not become distressed to the point that we become ineffective in ministry and unusable to Him.

We are troubled on every side, yet not distressed; we are perplexed, but not in despair; Persecuted, but not forsaken; cast down, but not destroyed; Always bearing about in the body the dying of the Lord Jesus, that the life also of Jesus might be made manifest in our body (2 Cor. 4:8–10).

Instructors need the Lord's instructions on how to think, react, and move in rejection situations. Jesus showed His disciples how to overcome rejection from people who should have been among His greatest supporters.

Jesus' main rejecters included those who lived in Nazareth, His hometown. To them, Jesus was just the carpenter's son. They knew the names of his mother and siblings, who still lived in the area. They would not accept that someone who lived among them could express such kingdom wisdom, do mighty works, and be the Messiah they waited for. Therefore, they rejected Jesus.

And they were offended in him. But Jesus said unto them, "A prophet is not without honour, save in his own country, and in his own house." And he did not many mighty works there because of their unbelief" (Matt. 13:57–58).

Many people in other places where Jesus taught had already made their decisions about His identity. They thought He was a past prophet who came back to life (Matt. 16:13–17).

Jesus did not allow people's perceptions, rejections, and misconceptions to distract Him from preaching and teaching about the kingdom of God.

As instructors, we, too, will face rejection from those unwilling to receive us beyond our family and hometown identities and beyond their perceptions. There are people so stuck on long-ago remembrances of us, they become offended that we no longer identify ourselves according to the past. They will not accept that we have grown beyond nicknames, high school and college reputations, and other descriptions of the past. They will insist on dealing with us according to the decisions *they* made about our identities. A number of them will go so far as to reject the instructions the Lord gives through us.

Therefore, we must ask our Lord to give us grace, peace, and patience so we are not stuck on becoming angry, offended, or bitter. Rather, we will continue to flow in our assignments as the Lord moves us through rejection and continues using us to instruct people willing to receive His wisdom. Instructors must know who God says they are and faithfully function according to those revelations.

So, leave the identity issue to God and focus on the name of the Great Instructor, who reigns forever.

> *Wherefore God also hath highly exalted him, and given him a name which is above every name: That at the name of Jesus every knee should bow, of things in heaven, and things in earth, and things under the earth; And that every tongue should confess that Jesus Christ is Lord, to the glory of God the Father* (Phil. 2:9–11).

Trusting that Jesus has won the victory over rejection, let us receive further instructions.

Rejection and Rebuke

During their ministry training, two of Jesus' disciples, James and John, found themselves in a tight spot between rejection and rebuke.

As detailed in Luke 9:51–53, Jesus was traveling to Jerusalem, where he would face his crucifixion. He sent messengers to Samaria to set up a place for Him and his disciples to rest. The townspeople refused them.

Samaria and Israel had a long-term history of hate between each other and thus were often unwelcoming toward one another. Not handling

Samaria's rejection in a Christ-like way, James and John offered their suggestion on how the issue could be resolved permanently.

> *And when his disciples James and John saw this, they said, "Lord, wilt thou that we command fire to come down from heaven, and consume them, even as Elias did?"* (Luke 9:54).

The brothers were referring to the Old Testament prophet Elijah, who—while in a showdown with false prophets at Mount Carmel—prayed for God's fire to come from heaven (1 Kings 18:21–39). The Lord honored Elijah's request, showing Himself to be the true God over false god Baal.

While Elijah wanted people to forsake idol worship and worship God, Jesus' disciples just wanted to punish Samaria. Angry about rejection and filled with pride, James and John wanted Samaria burned down. They wanted to command a move of God for their own purposes, feelings, and hatred.

Jesus would have none of that.

> *But he turned, and rebuked them, and said, "Ye know not what manner of spirit ye are of. For the Son of man is not come to destroy men's lives, but to save them." And they went to another village"* (Luke 9:55–56).

<u>There are three lessons instructors can learn from how Jesus, James, and John responded to this rejection experience.</u>

Lesson One: Be Aware of "What Manner of Spirit Ye Are of"

Jesus allowed the disciples to encounter a rejection situation to show them the conditions of their hearts.

Many times rejections come unexpectedly and harshly. Our responses show the condition of our hearts—the manner of spirit we are of, so to speak. Let us honestly assess how the conditions of our hearts affect us as instructors.

Do we hold grudges, get depressed, throw tantrums, or quit ministry or prayer groups? Do we try to push our ideas harder? Do we become competitive with other instructors?

Have we made unrighteous compromises in hopes of being accepted? Do we withhold giving messages from the Lord?

Do pride, frustrations, or prejudices affect our response to rejections?

Are there histories of hate in us concerning certain people, cultures, geographical settings, socioeconomic levels, or belief systems?

As James and John learned, instructors cannot have fits of self-will and use God's gifts, talents, and power to retaliate against rejection.

As instructors, we must be fully equipped with the fruit of the Spirit: love, joy, peace, long-suffering, gentleness, goodness, faith, meekness, and temperance (Gal. 5:22–23) as we mirror the attributes of our Almighty Instructor.

> *The Lord is merciful and gracious, slow to anger, and plenteous in mercy. He will not always chide: neither will he keep his anger for ever* (Ps. 103:8–9).

> *The Lord is gracious, and full of compassion; slow to anger, and of great mercy. The Lord is good to all: and his tender mercies are over all his works* (Ps. 145:8–9).

We must trust in the Lord's promises to handle vengeance on our behalf in accordance to His will and timing.

> *Dearly beloved, avenge not yourselves, but rather give place unto wrath: for it is written, "Vengeance is mine; I will repay," saith the Lord"* (Rom. 12:19).

> *For we know him that hath said, "Vengeance belongeth unto me, I will recompense," saith the Lord. And again, The Lord shall judge his people. It is a fearful thing to fall into the hands of the living God* (Heb. 10:30–31).

Lesson Two: Focus on the Lord's Movement in Rejection Situations

Jesus did not burn down Samaria or try to force his way in. He simply went another way. He led the disciples from a place of rejection through another village that provided passage.

Moving with the Lord prevents us from being stuck at rejections. There is more work to do and greater things to experience.

Kicked out of Antioch, teachers Paul and Barnabas shook the dust off their feet and went to another town, called Iconium, where the disciples "were filled with joy, and with the Holy Ghost" (Acts 13:50–51).

These get-up-and-go instructors were following the instructions of Jesus, who taught his disciples to move on after shaking the dust from their feet when they left a town that rejected them (Luke 9:5).

When there is a rejection, there must be a shaking. Shaking off the dust is a cleansing movement that keeps the rejection dirt from settling in the instructor's feet. In other words, the Lord is telling instructors, "Don't let rejection shake you. You shake it. I've given you instruction, power, and authority to shake the dirt off." We shake rejection by asking the Lord to revive us so we can continue to praise, worship, teach, and reach.

Remember, even Jesus experienced rejection though He healed the sick, raised the dead, miraculously fed thousands, and taught truths straight from the throne of God. We, too, will encounter rejections, no matter how much we teach, make sacrifices, pray, or wake up at 3 a.m. to listen or give counsel.

In John 4, Jesus ministered in Samaria; but in Luke 9, the town rejected Him. Sometimes, the same location will be the place of both great ministry and painful rejection.

Therefore, our focus is not on location, but on the Lord and His move. His work is still in motion. The Lord, through His people, is still saving, healing, delivering, and teaching.

Lesson Three: Don't Burn Your Assignment

James and John wanted to burn it. However, Jesus loved Samaria and wanted to save it. The disciples did not know Samaria would be part of their future ministry assignment.

> *"But ye shall receive power, after that the Holy Ghost is come upon you: and ye shall be witnesses unto me both in Jerusalem, and in all Judaea, and in Samaria, and unto the uttermost part of the earth"* (Acts 1:8).

Turns out, Jesus had kept his disciples from burning their assignment!

Experiencing rejection does not give us the right to burn our assignments. Some instructors have burned their assignments by quitting ministries or boycotting certain church activities in response to their rejection experiences.

There are instructors who have become proud and arrogant, ready to humiliate students not up to their standards. These instructors look down on ministries in which they are involved. Nothing others do or say is right, while they know all the answers.

Some instructors are still hurt, bitter, or unforgiving about a past rejection experience. They are suspicious and ready to fight or flee at the first sign of perceived trouble. While they feel they are protecting themselves, they actually are burning their assignments, making current students pay for things that happened in the past. Other instructors do not properly prepare for their teaching sessions, as they are resentful of students' patchy attendance habits.

Several instructors burn their assignments by being impatient and impolite to people they are assigned to. These instructors are high-minded, argumentative, and unwilling to listen.

There are instructors burning their assignments by not submitting to ministry leaders who determine curriculum. These instructors also are unsatisfied with teaching schedules, classroom sizes, and topics and materials associated with their assignments. They have more complaints about their assignments than revelations of what the Lord wants His students to learn. These instructors have become ineffective in the teaching ministry.

As results of their unwise actions and ungodly attitudes, several instructors have no students or ministry places. They burned down their assignments. Who or what will they complain about now?

> *Woe unto them that are wise in their own eyes, and prudent in their own sight!* (Isa. 5:21).

> *But he turned, and rebuked them, and said, "Ye know not what manner of spirit ye are of"* (Luke 9:55).

Don't Just Give It; Live It!

In 1 Kings 13, the Lord sent a prophet—referred to as a "man of God"—to deliver a message to a king. The Lord also healed the king as an answer to the prophet's prayer.

Prior to this, the Lord had given the prophet instructions, which the prophet repeated while declining an invitation to the king's home.

> *And the man of God said unto the king, "If thou wilt give me half thine house, I will not go in with thee ... For so was it charged me by the word of the Lord, saying, Eat no bread, nor drink water, nor turn again by the same way that thou camest." So he went another way, and returned not by the way that he came to Bethel* (1 Kings 13:8–10).

A short time later, the man of God received a dinner invitation from an older man. The man of God initially refused the offer, repeating the Lord's instructions. However, the encounter did not end there.

> *He said unto him, "I am a prophet also as thou art; and an angel spake unto me by the word of the Lord, saying, Bring him back with thee into thine house, that he may eat bread and drink water." But he lied unto him. So he went back with him, and did eat bread in his house, and drank water* (1 Kings 13:18–19).

The man of God had accepted the invitation of the persistent older man who identified himself as a prophet and turned out to be a liar. During the mealtime, a word from the Lord was given through the old prophet that the man of God would die because of his disobedience to instruction (1 Kings 13:20–22). A lion killed the man of God as he traveled from the old prophet's home (verse 24). He was buried in the grave of the old prophet, who instructed his sons that when he died, his body was to be put next to the man of God's remains (verses 29–31). The grave would testify of the disastrous results of disobedience and the tragic connection between the man of God and the old prophet.

<u>There are three lessons instructors can learn from</u>
<u>this man of God's ministry and downfall.</u>

Lesson One: Recognize the Significance of Practicing Careful and Complete Obedience

In 2 Corinthians 10:5, the apostle Paul tells the church to cast down arguments, teachings, and insights that are raised to challenge the knowledge of God, "bringing into captivity every thought to the obedience of Christ."

> *And having in readiness to revenge all disobedience, when your obedience is fulfilled* (2 Cor. 10:6).

Notice the phrase "when your obedience is fulfilled." Instructors must make sure they have fulfilled their obedience before they can effectively challenge disobedience in others.

> *Thou therefore which teachest another, teachest thou not thyself? thou that preachest a man should not steal, dost thou steal? Thou that sayest a man should not commit adultery, dost thou commit adultery? thou that abhorrest idols, dost thou commit sacrilege?* (Rom. 2:21–22).

While the prophet in 1 Kings 13 did deliver the Lord's message to the king, he did not fulfill his obedience concerning his own God-given instructions. Thus, he did not challenge, cast down, or revenge the words of disobedience that came from the old lying prophet.

As instructors, we must be careful to fulfill our obedience no matter what other words or reasoning people present us.

Lesson Two: Carefully and Prayerfully Consider Connections

We must be careful with opportunities to make connections with those who are "as thou art," the phrase used by the old, lying prophet in 1 Kings 13:18. While trying to convince the man of God to come to his home, the older man said that he, too, was a prophet with a word from God delivered by an angel.

Be careful of developing clique-like associations based on ministry assignments, titles, and positions. Indeed, we can gain insight from and develop connections with people who share similar ministry responsibilities or spiritual gifts. However, we cannot allow references to similar titles or assignments to deceive us into disobedience.

Again, an old prophet deceived the man of God. "Old" was not just indicative of his age, but of the extent of his faulty spiritual condition.

Some instructors are "old" in certain flaws or character issues, in that they have been that way for a long time. Their issues are deep-rooted, set-in, long-forgotten stains that have gone without cleansing and correction. While these instructors can hear and deliver instructions for others, they do not see or hear the corrections they need.

> *And why beholdest thou the mote that is in thy brother's eye, but considerest not the beam that is in thine own eye?... Thou hypocrite, first cast out the beam out of thine own eye; and then shalt thou see clearly to cast out the mote out of thy brother's eye* (Matt. 7:3, 5).

Lesson Three: Slow Down So You Can Live It

The third lesson to learn concerning careful and complete obedience is for instructors to slow down and allow the Lord to show them what to give out and when.

Some instructors are quickly producing material—books, videos, and study guides—filled with God-given teachings they have yet to obey themselves.

God gave several instructors revelations specifically meant for their own cleansing and correction. Rather than changing their ways, they turned into manufacturers, using God's revelations to push products. Therefore, we have still-arrogant and impatient instructors teaching others about humility and patience; unforgiving teachers selling products on forgiveness; crafty lecturers speaking about integrity and godly motives; and selfish spiritual mentors advising on how to share, serve, and give.

In 1 Corinthians 9:26–27, the apostle Paul wrote about his perseverance in being disciplined in and submitted to the teachings of the Gospel, "lest that by any means, when I have preached to others, I myself should be a castaway" (verse 27).

There are instructors with wonderful public ministries and great teaching material, while they have troubled private lives resulting from their unwise and ungodly character and behaviors.

Of course, the Lord has commissioned instructors to share His words through written works and multimedia methods. However, instructors still have an assignment to follow this instruction: "Don't just give it; live it."

> *For unto whomsoever much is given, of him shall be much required* (Luke 12:48).

Jesus warned of eternal consequences for those doing ministry work while they themselves are disobedient to His instructions:

> *"Not every one that saith unto me, 'Lord, Lord,' shall enter into the kingdom of heaven; but he that doeth the will of my Father which is in heaven. Many will say to me in that day, 'Lord, Lord, have we not prophesied in thy name? And in thy name have cast out devils? And in thy name done many wonderful works?' And then will I profess unto them, 'I never knew you: depart from me, ye that work iniquity'"* (Matt. 7:21–23).

Between a Rock and a Hard Place

Instructors faithful in doing the Lord's instructions can still find themselves between a rock and a hard place, as did Moses.

We find our next lesson in Numbers 20:1–13.

God assigned Moses to lead Israel out of slavery through the wilderness and into the Promised Land. After close to forty years in the wilderness, Moses stands between a rock and a multitude of hard-hearted people who are still disobedient and demanding. The children of Israel are out of water. As they have done throughout their journey, they complained. Moses was hard-pressed while being challenged by a nation of people often displeased by his efforts and the Lord's work. No matter how many miracles they received, they could not be satisfied.

Now everything was coming to a head at Kadesh, which means "be holy."[4] The pressure was massive, and the complaints were fast and furious. The nation's answer was going to flow through a rock, the last place anyone would expect to get water in abundance.

In the midst of Israel's complaining, Moses and his brother Aaron fell on their faces seeking the Lord's help. The glory of the Lord appeared. Then He gave them instructions.

> *"Take the rod, and gather thou the assembly together, thou, and Aaron thy brother, and speak ye unto the rock before their eyes; and it shall give forth his water, and thou shalt bring forth to them water out of the rock: so thou shalt give the congregation and their beasts drink." And Moses took the rod from before the Lord, as he commanded him* (Num. 20:8–9).

However, something still went wrong at the rock.

Instead of speaking to the rock as instructed, Moses began talking to the people, saying things the Lord did not tell him to say. He called them rebels (Num. 20:10). The more he talked, the angrier he got. Then he struck the rock twice. Water flowed out in abundance for the people and their animals (Num. 20:11).

Displeased by Moses' disobedience, the Lord gave him another instruction.

> *And the Lord spake unto Moses and Aaron, "Because ye believed me not, to sanctify me in the eyes of the children of Israel, therefore ye shall not bring this congregation into the land which I have given them"* (Num. 20:12).

There are four lessons instructors can learn from the rock incident.

Lesson One: Be Mindful of Spiritual Locations in Stressful Situations

As previously noted, the rock incident happened at Kadesh, which means "be holy." The location was indicative of what the Lord would manifest about Himself in the situation, as well as the standard of character He was expecting from the people, especially Moses and Aaron. The two leaders were to be examples to the complaining people of how to honor and show reverence to the Lord's holiness.

In Numbers 20:12, the Lord said Moses did not rely on His way of settling the matter according to His Holiness. Moses had "lifted up his hand," elevating his frustrations, authority (symbolized by the rod), strength, and will over the Lord's holy instructions.

While in difficult situations, instructors must remain focused on the holiness of God. He will get the glory as we obey His instructions in these situations. Frustrations cannot overshadow our holy responsibilities.

> *But as he which hath called you is holy, so be ye holy in all manner of conversation; Because it is written, "Be ye holy; for I am holy"* (1 Peter 1:15–16).

Lesson Two: Acknowledge the Truth of the Abundance

Let us review Numbers 20:11:

> *And Moses lifted up his hand, and with his rod he smote the rock twice: and the water came out abundantly, and the congregation drank, and their beasts also.*

Of course, the people were happy. They got what they wanted in abundance. However, the abundance came the wrong way. The people were wrong, and Moses was disobedient.

Abundant endings to situations do not mean all is right with the Lord. While He did give abundant water supply out of compassion for the people's needs, he still had a matter to settle with Moses afterward.

Instructors can have great endings to sermons or teaching sessions, hear testimonies of how their ministries helped people, or receive abundant supplies to their needs. Yet the Lord has a different view of the matter. While people see and celebrate great results, the Lord is looking for righteousness.

> *There is none as holy as the Lord: for there is none beside thee: neither is there any rock like our God. Talk no more so exceeding proudly; let not arrogancy come out of your mouth: for the Lord is a God of knowledge, and by him actions are weighed* (1 Sam. 2:2–3).

Remember, we can get an abundance of water and still not get the Promised Land.

Lesson Three: Behave

In Numbers 20:8–9, the Lord told Moses how to behave in the midst of the rock situation. He made comments that God did not authorize. Moses also struck a rock twice, rather than speaking to it as commanded. Moses had allowed his anger to take over. His behavior cost him the assignment to lead the people into the Promised Land.

Some instructors and leaders missed experiencing the great things the Lord had in store for them because of their wrong behaviors while being stuck between rocks and hard places. As instructors, we must wholeheartedly trust in God's way. We must be holy and behave.

These rocky places also are the miracle places where the Lord will manifest His Holy presence as He commands deliverances, healings, and supplies to flow out in abundance. Remember, instructors, we are not alone in these hard situations. The Lord is with us, ready to manifest His glory. He is our Rock.

> *The Lord is my rock, and my fortress, and my deliverer; The God of my rock; in him will I trust ... For who is God, save the Lord? and who is a rock, save our God?... The Lord liveth; and blessed be my rock; and exalted be the God of the rock of my salvation* (2 Sam. 22:2–3, 32, 47).

> *He only is my rock and my salvation: he is my defence; I shall not be moved. In God is my salvation and my glory: the rock of my strength, and my refuge, is in God* (Ps. 62:6–7).

> *Moreover, brethren, I would not that ye should be ignorant, how that all our fathers were under the cloud, and all passed through the sea; And were all baptized unto Moses in the cloud and in the sea; And did all eat the same spiritual meat; And did all drink the same spiritual drink: for they drank of that spiritual Rock that followed them: and that Rock was Christ* (1 Cor. 10:1–4).

Lesson Four: Move Beyond the Error

Though Moses fell short of the glory of God in Kadesh, he continued to lead God's people forward. He gave them instructions about their covenant with God and about their Promised Land responsibilities.

While Moses could not go into Canaan, the Lord did let him see the land. He also honored Moses' request to appoint another leader (Num. 27:12–22). The Lord chose Joshua, whom Moses consecrated for the work (verse 22).

Moses did not lose the Lord's love, relationship, or respect. After Moses' death, the Lord took care of his body and buried him (Deut. 34:5–6). The Lord included this tribute to Moses in Deuteronomy 34:10–12:

> *And there arose not a prophet since in Israel like unto Moses, whom the Lord knew face to face, In all the signs and the wonders, which the Lord sent him to do in the land of Egypt to Pharaoh, and to all his servants, and to all his land, And in all that mighty hand, and in all the great terror which Moses shewed in the sight of all Israel.*

The Lord is merciful, kind, and compassionate as He restores instructors who have failed or erred in their assignments.

Remember the apostle Peter. As a disciple, Peter repeatedly denied Jesus at the time of Jesus' crucifixion (Mark 14:66–72). However, after His death and resurrection, Jesus talked with Peter and restored him to ministry (John 21:15–17). Peter preached the Gospel on the Day of Pentecost, resulting in about three thousand souls receiving Jesus Christ as their Savior (Acts 2:14–41).

As the Great Instructor, the Lord corrects, not condemns. He moves us beyond our errors and shortcomings, enabling us to instruct again.

Instructors, Let Us Pray (from Ps. 51:1, 10–13, 15)

> *Have mercy upon me, O God, according to thy lovingkindness: according unto the multitude of thy tender mercies blot out my transgressions … Create in me a clean heart, O God; and renew a right spirit within me. Cast me not away from thy presence; and take not thy holy spirit from me. Restore unto me the joy of thy salvation; and uphold me with thy free spirit. Then will I teach transgressors thy ways; and sinners shall be converted unto thee … O Lord, open thou my lips; and my mouth shall shew forth thy praise. Amen.*

CHAPTER 16

Instructions for Instructors
Part II: From Humble Students to Powerful Leaders

The key to being a mature, obedient, and wise instructor is to remain a humble student.

> *He that refuseth instruction despiseth his own soul: but he that heareth reproof getteth understanding. The fear of the Lord is the instruction of wisdom; and before honour is humility* (Prov. 15:32–33).

Faithful students of God receive anointed, kingdom education through the guidance of the Holy Spirit, who dwells within us. He reveals to us the thoughts and instructions of God and guides us into all truth (John 16:13–15). Receiving the Lord's instructions through His Spirit and His appointed and anointed teachers will protect us from false teachings generated by human theories and speculations.

> *But the anointing which ye have received of him abideth in you, and ye need not that any man teach you: but as the same anointing teacheth you of all things, and is truth, and is no lie, and even as it hath taught you, ye shall abide in him* (1 John 2:27).

The Lord honors instructors who are willing to learn and receive correction when necessary, as they never stop being humble students at His feet.

Knowing that early-Church instructor Apollos was a humble student at heart, the Lord blessed him to receive complete understanding of the Gospel (Acts 18:24–28). The Lord could trust Apollos to readjust his teaching and life based on the things he learned. When Apollos humbly received instructions from the couple Aquila and Priscilla, the Lord blessed him with more ministry assignments.

Let us read our lesson Scripture from Acts 18:24–28:

> *And a certain Jew named Apollos, born at Alexandria, an eloquent man, and mighty in the Scriptures, came to Ephesus. This man was instructed in the way of the Lord; and being fervent in the spirit, he spake and taught diligently the things of the Lord, knowing only the baptism of John. And he began to speak boldly in the synagogue: whom when Aquila and Priscilla had heard, they took him unto them, and expounded unto him the way of God more perfectly. And when he was disposed to pass into Achaia, the brethren wrote, exhorting the disciples to receive him: who, when he was come, helped them much which had believed through grace: For he mightily convinced the Jews, and that publicly, shewing by the Scriptures that Jesus was Christ.*

<u>There are three lessons instructors can learn
from Apollos's learning experience.</u>

Lesson One: Be Aware of Opportunities to Receive Instruction Blessings from the Lord

While Apollos was an eloquent, diligent, and bold teacher, he lacked key information that prevented him from being a complete teacher. His knowledge was limited. He needed more instruction about Jesus.

As instructors, we may teach with impressive skills and pure motives to reach people for the Lord. However, some questions remain.

Are we lacking some information or insight? Do we have mature understanding of the material we are presenting? This is not about second-guessing oneself, but about getting in the student position so the Lord can bless us with more instructions.

When initially approached by Aquila and Priscilla, Apollos could have taken the attitude of "I already know the ways of the Lord." Do we have that attitude?

We must cast away pride and ego, and let the Lord be the expert. Then He will pour into us the wisdom and instructions He releases to humble students. Like Apollos, we are to take time to listen and learn. We don't know what the Lord is about to reveal next.

> *A wise man will hear, and will increase learning; and a man of understanding shall attain unto wise counsels* (Prov. 1:5).

> *Give instruction to a wise man, and he will be yet wiser: teach a just man, and he will increase in learning* (Prov. 9:9).

Apollos accepted the opportunity to receive additional training from Aquila and Priscilla, so they invested time, energy, and insight in him. They explained "the way of God more perfectly" (Acts 18:26).

The couple's student was not only a gifted teacher; he was good ground for the planting of more word.

> *But he that received seed into the good ground is he that heareth the word, and understandeth it; which also beareth fruit, and bringeth forth, some an hundredfold, some sixty, some thirty* (Matt. 13:23).

> *But that on the good ground are they, which in an honest and good heart, having heard the word, keep it, and bring forth fruit with patience* (Luke 8:15).

Blessed and equipped with complete understanding, Apollos had the backing of the Ephesian church, which wrote a letter endorsing his ministry when the time came for him to travel (Acts 18:27).

The all-knowing Lord had indeed blessed Apollos, supplying the instructor with essential information and support needed for complete ministry. The investment God made in Apollos catapulted the instructor's ministry.

*For he mightily convinced the Jews, and that publicly, shewing
by the Scriptures that Jesus was Christ* (Acts 18:28).

Lesson Two: *Learn from Aquila and Priscilla's Conduct as Instructors of the Instructor*

First, the couple listened with discernment to Apollos's presentation in the synagogue. They were able to hear beyond Apollos's extraordinary speaking skills and focus on the substance of his message.

Oftentimes, people are so impressed with oratory skills, they do not focus on the message. They hear boldness, delivery style, witty expressions, or big and flashy words, but not the message.

Aquila and Priscilla show the importance of not only weighing the substance of the message, but also knowing how to remain humble while assisting other instructors who need additional understanding.

Having heard Apollos's limitations in his knowledge of the Lord, Aquila and Priscilla did not attempt to downgrade, humiliate, or disregard him. They did not dismiss Apollos's teaching ministry as useless. They did not intimidate him or publicly question him to expose his limitations. Recognizing that Apollos truly wanted to teach for the Lord, the couple simply committed themselves to helping him grow spiritually.

As Aquila and Priscilla took time to explain the complete message of the Gospel, they and other Ephesian church members developed a fellowship with Apollos. This close fellowship developed because of their humility to the Lord, to His instructions, and to each other.

Aquila and Priscilla showed the great works the Lord accomplishes through humble teachers who honestly and effectively instruct humble students.

Lesson Three: *Focus on Christ to Avoid Contentions, Competitions, Comparisons, and Conceit*

Let us review Acts 18:27–28 to see the results of Apollos receiving instructions from Aquila and Priscilla:

*And when he was disposed to pass into Achaia, the brethren
wrote, exhorting the disciples to receive him: who, when he
was come, helped them much which had believed through*

grace: For he mightily convinced the Jews, and that publicly,
shewing by the Scriptures that Jesus was Christ.

The Lord blessed Apollos with a power-packed teaching ministry that produced incredible results. Apollos's popularity increased as his ministry grew.

However, a troubling trend was growing in the early church. People began focusing more on the instructors than the instructions. As a result, their fellowship with one another became threatened. They argued over following favorite teachers and preachers. Contentions grew as boasting about servants overshadowed praising the Savior.

The apostle Paul addressed the issue with the church in Corinth:

> *For it hath been declared unto me of you, my brethren,*
> *by them which are of the house of Chloe, that there are*
> *contentions among you. Now this I say, that every one of*
> *you saith, "I am of Paul; and I of Apollos; and I of Cephas;*
> *and I of Christ." Is Christ divided? was Paul crucified for*
> *you? or were ye baptized in the name of Paul?* (1 Cor.
> 1:11–13).

Through his response to the "favorite teacher/preacher" issue, Paul showed that instructors are not to relish in people-generated popularity, nor are people to focus squarely on instructors. Paul challenged his readers to drop their flesh-driven favoritism arguments and become mature in the Lord. The apostle reminded them that Christ is the foundation and focus of ministry and God gets the glory for every spiritual success.

God knows how to orchestrate the instruction ministries He commissions. He uses these ministries to do what He pleases in those He reaches.

> *For while one saith, "I am of Paul"; and another, "I am*
> *of Apollos"; are ye not carnal? Who then is Paul, and who*
> *is Apollos, but ministers by whom ye believed, even as the*
> *Lord gave to every man? I have planted, Apollos watered;*
> *but God gave the increase ... Now he that planteth and*
> *he that watereth are one ... For we are labourers together*
> *with God* (1 Cor. 3:4–9).

Instructors must acknowledge and appreciate how God puts His people together to complete great work in churches, communities, and nations. However, there are instructors who need God to cleanse them of desires to be popular. These conceited instructors love to compete and compare. They are boasters of their own works. They present their work as being more creative, innovative, productive, or advanced than other ministries in their communities or church organizations. These instructors are more dedicated to their ministry names, visions, and buildings, than to their purposes within the Body of Christ. They attempt to function as the mouth of the Body, not considering they might be the toes responsible for maintaining stability when the rest of the foot elevates. In other words, their assignments are to support and serve other instructors the Lord brings to the forefront for specific ministry duties at specific times.

Several instructors compete against each other, though they are members of the same congregation. Forgetting there is a vast vineyard of souls needing instructions, these instructors remain stuck to church buildings, fighting over teaching ministries, including Sunday school, Bible study, and youth classes. To overcome these issues, instructors need to study these verses:

> For I say, through the grace given unto me, to every man that is among you, not to think of himself more highly than he ought to think ... For as we have many members in one body, and all members have not the same office: So we, being many, are one body in Christ, and every one members one of another ... Be kindly affectioned one to another with brotherly love; in honour preferring one another (Rom. 12:3–5, 10).

> Yea, all of you be subject one to another, and be clothed with humility: for God resisteth the proud, and giveth grace to the humble. Humble yourselves therefore under the mighty hand of God, that he may exalt you in due time (1 Peter 5:5–6).

Like fellow instructors Peter and Apollos, Paul understood the responsibilities, sacrifices, and value of being a humble student.

In Philippians 3:4–10, Paul said he could revel in self-confidence due to his family history of being from the same Benjamin tribe as King Saul, Israel's first ruler. Paul, a former church persecutor, said he also could boast about his top-notch education, as well as his high religious and social ranking from his Pharisee days. However, the apostle had cast all that aside, esteeming the knowledge of Christ to be greater than the accomplishments.

The apostle Paul also endured a ministry climate where instructors' motives were not always honorable. During Paul's imprisonment for preaching the Gospel, several ministers amped up their own preaching efforts, though for different reasons.

> *Some indeed preach Christ even of envy and strife; and some also of good will: The one preach Christ of contention, not sincerely, supposing to add affliction to my bonds: But the other of love, knowing that I am set for the defence of the gospel* (Phil. 1:15–17).

However, the apostle did not harbor hostility toward instructors who were merely opportunists trying to capitalize on his unpleasant situation. He did not become jealous of righteous instructors who continued to preach freely. Paul kept his focus on Christ, a mature move that kept him in the right spirit, giving him the correct and joy-filled response to the issue.

> *What then? notwithstanding, every way, whether in pretence, or in truth, Christ is preached; and I therein do rejoice, yea, and will rejoice* (Phil. 1:18).

Let Us Pray

Lord, cleanse us of conceit and competitiveness. Forgive us for making comparisons between ministries You commissioned. Thank You for showing us the significance of remaining Your humble students in order to become mature instructors.

Lord, our focus is on You. We are depending on You to show us powerful and fruitful ministry paths as we commit to develop into the instructors You created us to be. Amen.

Left to Lead

There are several instances in the Bible where individuals or groups received callings to continue the godly work of their previous leaders.

After Moses' death, Joshua was left to lead the nation of Israel into Canaan (Josh. 1:1–11).

As the prophet Elijah was carried to heaven in a chariot of fire, his spiritual apprentice, Elisha, looked on, left to pick up the ministry mantle (2 Kings 2:11–14).

After Jesus returned to heaven, His disciples were left to continue His ministry (Mark 16:15–19).

While approaching his time of martyrdom, the apostle Paul urged a young pastor named Timothy to faithfully continue the work of preaching the Gospel (2 Tim. 4:1–7).

Before that, Paul had trained another young instructor, Titus, for missionary work. We will focus on Titus's left-to-lead experience to learn how the Lord provides order through His instructors.

Paul assigned Titus to an island situated in the Mediterranean Sea, about a thousand miles from Jerusalem.

> *For this cause left I thee in Crete, that thou shouldest set in order the things that are wanting, and ordain elders in every city, as I had appointed thee* (Titus 1:5).

Left in Crete, Titus had no easy escape from a less-than-ideal ministry situation. His assignment was to bring order to a chaotic church environment that mirrored its societal surroundings:

> *For there are many unruly and vain talkers and deceivers, specially they of the circumcision: Whose mouths must be stopped, who subvert whole houses, teaching things which they ought not, for filthy lucre's sake. One of themselves, even a prophet of their own, said, "the Cretians are alway liars, evil beasts, slow bellies." This witness is true ... They profess that they know God; but in works they deny him, being abominable, and disobedient, and unto every good work reprobate* (Titus 1:10–13, 16).

Let us face it. There are times when the Lord will not let instructors leave, no matter how chaotic the situations. Some instructors are doing their best to escape. They have yet to realize that bringing order to the chaos is their assignment. These instructors have been left to lead.

<u>There are three lessons instructors can learn
from Titus's left-to-lead experience.</u>

Lesson One: We Cannot Boycott Assignments that Require Exposure to Disorder

Several instructors are boycotting certain ministry groups, classes, and programs, planning to return only when "they get their act together."

Guess who God is calling to get their act together—these instructors.

Having his act together is what qualified Titus to lead and bring order in chaotic Crete. Paul trained Titus on how to remain in order spiritually and behaviorally while addressing chaotic issues.

The church in Crete had some serious problems, but boycotting it was not the answer. The solution came through sending an obedient and powerful instructor equipped to restore order. The apostle Paul did not mince words while informing Titus of the troublesome spiritual, behavioral, and societal issues involved in the Crete situation.

The Lord used a similar forewarning method while calling Ezekiel to prophetic ministry. He told Ezekiel the assignment would be to minister to "stiffhearted" and "most rebellious" people (Ezek. 2:3–7). The people's issues did not excuse Ezekiel from doing the Lord's work. The prophet was being sent to people because they were stiff-hearted and rebellious, which the Lord was willing to work through because of His love and relationship desires for them.

When the Lord uses instructors to restore order, they first must be exposed to chaos.

Some instructors have yet to learn this lesson, as they are quick to get bent out of shape when their microphones aren't functioning correctly or their students are late or other teachers went over their allotted time or not everything was properly organized or ... well, the list goes on. These instructors can learn from people in professions that require exposure to the horrendous in order to give the help.

Physicians have to inspect and touch infected areas to know how to treat their patients. Firefighters run into burning buildings to battle flames or rescue those who are yet inside. Police go into disturbing crime scenes to conduct investigations that help get justice for victims. Coroners examine bodies in horrible conditions to find causes of death or find clues that will help solve homicide cases. Soldiers are exposed to enemy fighters and weapons while battling to win wars.

Instructors must be willing to endure exposure to chaotic and unpleasant conditions—whether from foreign missions or local ministry work—for them to be in the right godly position to restore order.

Lesson Two: Seek the Lord's Specific Instructions on How to Handle Assignments

In his letter to Titus, Apostle Paul advised:

> *Wherefore rebuke them sharply, that they may be sound in the faith* (Titus 1:13).

Rebuking the Cretians meant boldly calling attention to their wrong words, behaviors, spiritual conditions, and attitudes, while presenting them truth and casting down the lies. Titus could not tolerate excuses, practices, or teachings that did not meet the standard of holiness. He had to get the Cretians to come face-to-face with their wrongs and convince them to acknowledge and renounce their sins.

Titus had to do this sharply, Paul said. This did not give Titus permission to be rude or callous to people. He had to be sharp as the Word of God is sharp, able to discern thoughts, motives, and plans of the heart (Heb. 4:12). Titus had to get to the heart of the Crete issue. He had to operate in the spirit like a heart surgeon cutting through skin and rib cage to get access to the sickly, blood-pumping organ.

Surgeons are trained to use sharp instruments and acute skills to correct cardiac conditions without killing their patients. Though surgeons use sharp instruments, their motives are to restore health and proper function to hearts.

The Lord, our Great Physician, trains instructors to correct the heart of chaotic issues without making people feel worthless or killing their opportunities to grow into spiritually healthy disciples.

By having Titus assigned to them, the Crete church members received opportunities to repent of their sins, renew their relationship with God and each other, and grow together in the faith.

For Titus, the true motive for rebuking the chaotic Cretians sharply was to help them become "sound in faith" (Titus 1:13). This meant becoming stable in the Lord's doctrine, orderly in ministry work, holy in everyday life, godly in words and thoughts, and righteous in motives.

Some instructors are not getting these assignment results, as they only go into rebuke-sharply mode because of frustration and impatience with the chaotic situations. These instructors become rude, overbearing, and controlling. Several of them go into micromanaging mode. They are bringing more confusion to the chaos.

Several irritated instructors have dared to stage coups against the Lord's plans. They are imposing their own will and treating people the way they see fit. They need to consider the instructions the Lord gave Ezekiel about remaining faithful despite the rebellion of others:

> *"And thou shalt speak my words unto them, whether they will hear, or whether they will forbear: for they are most rebellious. But thou, son of man, hear what I say unto thee; Be not thou rebellious like that rebellious house: open thy mouth, and eat that I give thee"* (Ezek. 2:7–8).

As instructors called to restore order in Crete-like situations, we must open our mouths to the Lord and let Him put His words in us. Then we will know how to speak when we must rebuke, correct, and restore.

Lesson Three: The Lord Can Lead Through Instructors Who Are Not in Charge

Oftentimes, instructors are serving in ministries and programs where leaders are part of the chaotic issues. These leaders may lack the skills, qualifications, or commitment to bring order to the problems. In these cases, the Lord wisely uses instructors to show leaders how to do things "decently and in order" (1 Cor. 14:40).

This does not mean the Lord will promote instructors or allow them to take over. Rather, the Lord has a way of moving through His instructors to have them handle their assignments excellently and without confusion. Then the souls involved in chaotic issues will still receive His ministry despite the circumstances. The Lord's order will flow through His instructors and permeate the atmosphere, making it conducive to receive His work.

Among us are instructors wondering why the Lord is taking so long to grant their requests for order. They have yet to realize they are the answers to their order prayers. They are the "Tituses" the Lord has left to lead.

CHAPTER 17

Instructions for Instructors
Part III: Beautiful Ministry

As we learned through the Titus-Crete situation, instructors must be patient, committed, and obedient enough for God to use them to bring beauty to ugly situations.

As instructors, we can pray that the beauty of the Lord be upon us and on the work He gives us to complete (Ps. 90:17). This beauty is the manifestation of the Lord's glorious presence, which refreshes and revives souls. This beauty also brings indescribable peace to troubled minds; healing to lives and relationships; and hope, relief, and joy to the brokenhearted.

Beautiful results flow from instruction ministries filled with the Lord's beauty:

> *The Spirit of the Lord GOD is upon me; because the Lord hath anointed me to preach good tidings unto the meek ... To appoint unto them that mourn in Zion, to give unto them beauty for ashes, the oil of joy for mourning, the garment of praise for the spirit of heaviness; that they might be called trees of righteousness, the planting of the Lord, that he might be glorified* (Isa. 61:1, 3).

Notice how "them that mourn" gain strength and flourish into "trees of righteousness, the planting of the Lord." They begin to function according to the beauty ministered to them.

> *And they shall build the old wastes, they shall raise up the former desolations, and they shall repair the waste cities, the desolations of many generations* (Isa. 61:4).

In Acts 3:1–11, a beautiful thing happened at the gate called Beautiful, which was outside the temple in Jerusalem. The apostles Peter and John were on their way into the temple to pray when a man who was unable to walk asked them for alms.

> *Then Peter said, "Silver and gold have I none; but such as I have give I thee: In the name of Jesus Christ of Nazareth rise up and walk." And he took him by the right hand, and lifted him up: and immediately his feet and ankle bones received strength. And he leaping up stood, and walked, and entered with them into the temple, walking, and leaping, and praising God. And all the people saw him walking and praising God* (Acts 3:6–9).

What beautiful instructions has the Lord imparted to us to bring healing, freedom, and leaping joy to those in need of His touch and ministry? As instructors, we need to take beauty classes from the Lord, learning about the beauty techniques, beauty treatments, and beauty supplies He has in store for those who receive His instructions.

> *One thing have I desired of the Lord, that will I seek after; that I may dwell in the house of the Lord all the days of my life, to behold the beauty of the Lord, and to enquire in his temple* (Ps. 27:4).

<u>The Lord has beautiful ministry to encourage, fortify, and bless His instructors.</u>

The Lord Honors Our Sacrifices

To the instructors who sacrifice much and rarely receive appreciation, please know that the Lord delights in you and cherishes your work in His kingdom.

> *Therefore, my beloved brethren, be ye stedfast, unmoveable, always abounding in the work of the Lord, forasmuch as ye know that your labour is not in vain in the Lord* (1 Cor. 15:58).

> *We give thanks to God always for you all, making mention of you in our prayers; Remembering without ceasing your work of faith, and labour of love, and patience of hope in our Lord Jesus Christ, in the sight of God and our Father* (1 Thess. 1:2–3)

> *For God is not unrighteous to forget your work and labour of love, which ye have shewed toward his name, in that ye have ministered to the saints, and do minister* (Heb. 6:10).

> *"And, behold, I come quickly; and my reward is with me, to give every man according as his work shall be"* (Rev. 22:12).

The Lord Is with Us in Times of Rejections

To instructors who experience rejection or ostracism, know that the Lord's companionship and love for you are everlasting.

> *Surely goodness and mercy shall follow me all the days of my life: and I will dwell in the house of the Lord for ever* (Ps. 23:6).

> *When my father and my mother forsake me, then the Lord will take me up* (Ps. 27:10).

> *"Go ye therefore, and teach all nations, baptizing them in the name of the Father, and of the Son, and of the Holy Ghost: Teaching them to observe all things whatsoever I*

have commanded you: and, lo, I am with you always, even unto the end of the world. Amen" (Matt. 28:19–20).

The Lord Understands Our Need for Rest

To instructors who are tired, overworked, or burned out, know that the Lord understands. He has the rest you need to revive, refresh, and reinvigorate you.

> *And he said, "My presence shall go with thee, and I will give thee rest"* (Ex. 33:14).

> *We have sought the Lord our God … and he hath given us rest on every side* (2 Chron. 14:7).

> *He maketh me to lie down in green pastures: he leadeth me beside the still waters. He restoreth my soul* (Ps. 23:2–3).

> *"Come unto me, all ye that labour and are heavy laden, and I will give you rest. Take my yoke upon you, and learn of me; for I am meek and lowly in heart: and ye shall find rest unto your souls"* (Matt. 11:28–29).

> *And the apostles gathered themselves together unto Jesus, and told him all things, both what they had done, and what they had taught. And he said unto them, "Come ye yourselves apart into a desert place, and rest a while"* (Mark 6:30–31).

The Lord Hears Our Prayers for Wisdom

To instructors crying out to the Lord for more wisdom and instructions, know that He promises to answer your prayers.

> *Yea, if thou criest after knowledge, and liftest up thy voice for understanding; If thou seekest her as silver, and searchest for her as for hid treasures; Then shalt thou understand the fear of the Lord, and find the knowledge of God. For the Lord giveth wisdom: out of his mouth cometh knowledge and understanding* (Prov. 2:3–6).

"Call unto me, and I will answer thee, and show thee great and mighty things, which thou knowest not" (Jer. 33:3).

If any of you lack wisdom, let him ask of God, that giveth to all men liberally, and upbraideth not; and it shall be given him (James 1:5).

The Lord Will Successfully Work Through Us

To instructors who have become discouraged, wondering whether they are doing a good job or whether they can do the job at all, remember the Lord has called you and equipped you for His work. Have faith in His favorable thoughts concerning you. Trust Him to do His work through you.

"Fear thou not; for I am with thee: be not dismayed; for I am thy God: I will strengthen thee; yea, I will help thee; yea, I will uphold thee with the right hand of my righteousness" (Isa. 41:10).

Now unto him that is able to do exceeding abundantly above all that we ask or think, according to the power that worketh in us (Eph. 3:20).

Wherefore also we pray always for you, that our God would count you worthy of this calling, and fulfil all the good pleasure of his goodness, and the work of faith with power: That the name of our Lord Jesus Christ may be glorified in you, and ye in him, according to the grace of our God and the Lord Jesus Christ (2 Thess. 1:11–12).

For it is God which worketh in you both to will and to do of his good pleasure (Phil. 2:13).

Beautiful from Head to Toe

As the Head of our instruction ministries, Jesus deeply cares for our physical, emotional, and spiritual well-being. He knows the challenges we face and knows how to nurture every part of us. He misses nothing.

The Lord admires the feet of His servants who faithfully deliver His words.

> *How beautiful upon the mountains are the feet of him that bringeth good tidings, that publisheth peace; that bringeth good tidings of good, that publisheth salvation; that saith unto Zion, "Thy God reigneth"* (Isa. 52:7).

> *As it is written, "How beautiful are the feet of them that preach the gospel of peace, and bring glad tidings of good things!"* (Rom. 10:15).

The Lord is the Head who refreshes, nurtures, and beautifies us right down to our toes.

Just hours away from his crucifixion, Jesus demonstrated His love and care for his disciples. He washed their feet, which was customary for house servants to do in their time (John 13:1–5).

> *So after he had washed their feet ... he said unto them, "Know ye what I have done to you? Ye call me Master and Lord: and ye say well; for so I am. If I then, your Lord and Master, have washed your feet; ye also ought to wash one another's feet"* (John 13:12–14).

Jesus' commands for the disciples to wash one another's feet meant they were to serve and comfort each other just as He had done for them.

Instructors today have the beautiful responsibility to receive the Lord's comfort and share it with each other.

> *Blessed be God, even the Father of our Lord Jesus Christ, the Father of mercies, and the God of all comfort; Who comforteth us in all our tribulation, that we may be able to comfort them which are in any trouble, by the comfort wherewith we ourselves are comforted of God ... And our hope of you is stedfast, knowing, that as ye are partakers of the sufferings, so shall ye be also of the consolation* (2 Cor. 1:3–4, 7).

Beautiful Moments with the Lord

Instructors, be comforted as the Lord soothes you in appreciation of your obedience, sacrifices, and endurances of hardships.

You have done what the Lord asked of you. Trust Him with the results. Wait on the Lord to manifest the wonderful effects of your ministry. He makes everything beautiful in its time (Eccl. 3:11).

Humbly appreciate how precious you are to the Lord. In Him, you are beautiful from head to toe. His glory, grace, and presence are your beautiful garments.

Praise the Lord and thank Him for choosing, equipping, and using you for His glory. Worship him in the beauty of holiness (Ps. 29:2).

Release every concern, worry, and weariness to the Lord as He pours His beauty, love, and strength upon you. Take nice, deep breaths in His beautiful presence. Recline in Him. Smile as you meditate on His goodness and greatness.

Enjoy your beautiful moments with the Lord.

> *Whom have I in heaven but thee? and there is none upon earth that I desire beside thee. My flesh and my heart faileth: but God is the strength of my heart, and my portion for ever ... it is good for me to draw near to God: I have put my trust in the Lord GOD, that I may declare all thy works* (Ps. 73:25–26, 28).

CHAPTER 18

Battle Instructions
Part I: Strategies, Sins, and Wins

The Lord's strategy is the key to winning battles. Through His strategy, we learn when, where, who, and how to battle, or whether we should go into battle at all. The Lord has already shown us who our real enemies are and where the battle lies.

> *Finally, my brethren, be strong in the Lord, and in the power of his might. Put on the whole armour of God, that ye may be able to stand against the wiles of the devil. For we wrestle not against flesh and blood, but against principalities, against powers, against the rulers of the darkness of this world, against spiritual wickedness in high places* (Eph. 6:10–12).

Our Lord is strong and mighty in battle (Ps. 24:8). He is our "battle ax" and weapon of war (Jer. 51:20). He breaks in pieces every plan, equipment, and resource Satan and his cohorts attempt to use against us. The enemy's weapons will not prosper against us (Isa. 54:17).

When Jesus spoke of building His church, He declared that the gates of hell would not prevail against it (Matt. 16:18).

The apostle Paul wrote that despite insistent persecution against the early church, there was nothing the enemy could do to separate Christians from the almighty love of God (Rom. 8:31–38). As a matter of fact, the church continued to grow and spread as Christians—scattered while escaping persecution—continued preaching and developing fellowships wherever they went (Acts 8:3–4 and James 1:1).

We cannot let battle situations stifle us. We can still grow, increase in wisdom and love, and abound in the Lord's work of bringing souls into His kingdom.

The Lord will use our battle situations to show others that He is the caring Savior and Mighty Deliverer, who has victories in store for those who rely on Him. We recognize that the Lord is our victory when we follow His battle instructions.

When the Lord Says "Go" or "No"

Throughout the Bible, the Lord has shown Himself to be the all-powerful and undefeatable Warrior. Those who sought and obeyed His counsel and strategies experienced great success. Those who were disobedient suffered devastating losses.

Israel's King David took various battle situations to the Lord. David did not take for granted that the Lord would give the same strategy each time.

In 1 Chronicles 14, the king faced a battle situation with the Philistines. He asked the Lord whether he should "go up" (advance) against the Philistines and whether he would win against them (verse 10).

The Lord replied, "Go up," giving David permission to fight, assuring the king's victory. After his combat win, the king gave glory to the Lord, recognizing Him as the breakthrough of the battle.

> So they came up to Baalperazim; and David smote them there. Then David said, "God hath broken in upon mine enemies by mine hand like the breaking forth of waters": therefore they called the name of that place Baalperazim. And when they had left their gods there, David gave a commandment, and they were burned with fire (1 Chron. 14:11–12).

However, the war was not over. In attempts to avenge their defeat, the Philistines came up for war again (1 Chron. 14:13). David again asked the Lord whether to go out against them. This time the Lord replied, "Go not up." He gave David a different strategy, which led Israel to another victory.

> *Therefore David enquired again of God; and God said unto him, "Go not up after them; turn away from them, and come upon them over against the mulberry trees. And it shall be, when thou shalt hear a sound of going in the tops of the mulberry trees, that then thou shalt go out to battle: for God is gone forth before thee to smite the host of the Philistines"* (1 Chron. 14:14–15).

Though David faced the same enemy in the same area, the Lord used two different strategies to deal with an issue that seemed to be the same old battle.

We, too, must seek the Lord's approach for every phase of war against the enemy. We need to know when the Lord says, "Go" or "No."

The Lord is the Great General, who teaches us how to fight and how to use His weapons of victory (Ps. 18:34–35). The Lord is our strategy, our first line of defense, and the Victorious One who leads the charge.

Are we asking the Lord for His strategy for our enemy situations? Do we know what spiritual weapons to use and how? Do we know which Scriptures to apply, how to pray, or whether to call a prayer partner?

Should we stand up, stand back, or stand still? Should we "Go up" or "Go not up"?

Remember how David was told to wait for the shaking of the mulberry tree as a sign of the Lord's moving before him to prepare the battlefield for Israel's victory (1 Chron. 14:14–15). Have we waited for the Lord to shake something in our situations? Has He given a word, confirmation, or some other go-ahead sign for our involvement in battles?

Many people will discern the enemy's operations and then charge into war against him. Some people are legitimate, God-sent battlers; others are merely self-driven meddlers. The difference between battlers and meddlers is the Lord's instructions.

Several leaders have downgraded themselves from legitimate battlers to defeated meddlers because they have stopped going to the Lord for war-by-war strategies. They handle current battles according to past war experiences. Battlers receive commands, strategies, and wisdom from the Lord to get involved. Meddlers think their life experiences, titles, and ideas give them the right to intervene. Their minds are so stuck on getting involved, they ignore the Lord's instructions to stay clear.

In 2 Chronicles 35:20–25, King Josiah ignored warnings not to meddle in a war that did not involve his nation, Judah. Egypt and Assyria were teaming up to fight against Babylon. To get to the war zone, Egyptian soldiers followed their king's command to march through Judah, a move King Josiah was trying to stop.

Let us read more about this situation:

> *After all this, when Josiah had prepared the temple, Necho king of Egypt came up to fight against Charchemish by Euphrates: and Josiah went out against him. But he sent ambassadors to him, saying, "What have I to do with thee, thou king of Judah? I come not against thee this day, but against the house wherewith I have war: for God commanded me to make haste: forbear thee from meddling with God, who is with me, that he destroy thee not"* (2 Chron. 35:20–21).

Note the timing of this war.

Josiah had spent years purging idols from his nation, while leading people back into a covenant relationship with the Lord. He also led the renovation of the temple. There was great revival in the land. Having experienced such a powerful spiritual turnaround nationwide, Josiah may have become overconfident in his decision to engage an enemy army.

How many of us have become supercharged after powerful revival experiences, so assured of victory that we rushed into battle situations without consulting God? We assumed the revival was preparing us for the battle. We did not realize that God gave us this wonderful spiritual experience to draw us closer to Him, so we could hear Him say, "Don't meddle. Do not get into that battle. You're not going to win that way."

Josiah received a no-meddling warning from God through an ungodly ruler of Egypt, a country that had once enslaved the people of

Israel. This was a good time to verify the warning with God since the source seemed questionable: "Lord, this is what I'm hearing from the enemy, but what do you say?"

The prophet Jeremiah was ministering in Judah at that time. The king could have gone to him for further insight on the matter. Instead, Josiah meddled.

> *Nevertheless Josiah would not turn his face from him, but disguised himself, that he might fight with him, and hearkened not unto the words of Necho from the mouth of God, and came to fight in the valley of Megiddo* (2 Chron. 35:22).

Josiah disguised himself because he decided not to listen to counsel that truly was coming from "the mouth of God." Josiah tried to hide from the enemy, but he could not hide from the warning of God.

We cannot disguise ourselves or hide our motives from the mouth of God. His words are our victory. Seeking the Lord's strategy is more important than going after the enemy. With his mind set on what he wanted to do, Josiah went into war. This great king suffered a tragic end:

> *And the archers shot at king Josiah; and the king said to his servants, "Have me away; for I am sore wounded" ... and they brought him to Jerusalem, and he died, and was buried in one of the sepulchres of his fathers. And all Judah and Jerusalem mourned for Josiah. And Jeremiah lamented for Josiah* (2 Chron. 35:23–25).

There are battles going on around us, and we need help. Have we sought the mouth of God concerning these matters? Are there warnings we are not heeding? Do we have the Lord's authorization to go into these battles? Did the Lord say "Go" or "No"?

Ahab, king of Israel, and Jehoshaphat, king of Judah, both were told "No" when they asked the prophet Micaiah about their plans to join forces to go into battle against Syria, a common enemy that occupied Israel's territory, Ramothgilead (2 Chron. 18).

Ahab's false prophets initially told the kings they would be victorious. While Ahab was content to hear these false claims, Jehoshaphat asked for a true word from the Lord. Ahab told Jehoshaphat about Micaiah. Ahab said he hated Micaiah because Micaiah "never prophesied good unto me, but always evil" (2 Chron. 18:7). Summoned by the two kings, Micaiah told them that the other prophets were lying. He prophesied that there would be no victory at Ramothgilead and Ahab would die in battle (2 Chron. 18:16–27).

The two kings went to war anyway, with Ahab disguising himself. He was killed by a randomly shot arrow (2 Chron. 18:33–34).

Prior to that, Jehoshaphat almost lost his life in the war. Enemy soldiers who had orders to kill Israel's king had surrounded him. They thought Jehoshaphat—dressed in his kingly garb—was Ahab. When Jehoshaphat cried out for his life, the Lord intervened, causing the soldiers to move away (Chron. 18:31).

The Lord later rebuked Jehoshaphat for making an allegiance with Ahab (2 Chron. 19:2). Ahab was a wicked king who surrounded himself with people who fed his ego and confirmed his godless plans. He would not accept "No" for an answer, even from God. Rather than repenting of his evil ways, Ahab harbored resentment against Micaiah. Ahab paid a tragic price for his habitual disobedience.

Iniquity sets in our hearts when we refuse to heed the Lord's "No" concerning relationship, financial, church, career, and other plans. Some of us do not like hearing the words "No," "Not yet," "Slow down," or "Wait." We want to be progressive, unstoppable, ever-victorious Christians on the move. Thus, phrases of warning, waiting, caution, or stop come across as fearful, faithless, defeated, and stagnant.

The Lord has given us people like Micaiah. They are courageous enough to stand up to a congregation, a board of trustees, or a group of ministers, and say, "The Lord said, 'No. This is not My strategy, and no victory will come through it.'"

In response, disobedient groups will push the Micaiahs to the side. These groups will attempt to disguise their plans by reworking details, changing locations, holding secretly rescheduled meetings, or bringing in more gifted or financially viable people. They are going ahead with their plans, while their lying prophets cheer them on.

The Lord is saying "No" to protect them from their enemies and from defeat. They think they are the good ones of the Gospel and are convinced they will not lose to the enemy.

Note the similarities between good revival-leading King Josiah and evil King Ahab. Both kings disregarded the Lord's "No." Then they went into battle thinking their disguises would hide and protect them. God's words—and the enemies' arrows—found them.

Overcoming Battle Sins

Kings Josiah and Ahab both sinned in not obeying God's instructions concerning their battle issues.

We all have sinned during battle times. We made ill-advised investments. We mishandled problems. We do have incredible battle victories and testimonies. However, we still suffer some losses because we are not consistent in following the Lord's instructions.

Some of us are battling debt because we did not obey the Lord's instructions about saving money or correcting spending habits.

Others are battling marital and family issues because they want their ways and traditions to be right, rather than follow the Lord's instructions on what will actually work for their specific households. Several people are going through marriage problems because they ignored the Lord's instruction not to marry that person in the first place or because they were too quick to run to the altar, not giving the Lord time to prepare them or their future spouses for their unions.

Many people are battling health issues because they ignored the Lord's instructions to eat properly, exercise, or see a doctor about nagging pains or ongoing health conditions.

There are pastors battling to keep their church doors open because they lost focus of the reasons the Lord called their churches into existence in the first place. These pastors have moved away from praying, fasting, and spending time in the Lord's presence. They emphasize their own agenda and visions, rather than submit to the strategies of the Lord.

We all have to recognize and repent of our battle sins.

> *For all have sinned, and come short of the glory of God* (Rom. 3:23).

> *If we say that we have no sin, we deceive ourselves, and the truth is not in us. If we confess our sins, he is faithful and just to forgive us our sins, and to cleanse us from all unrighteousness. If we say that we have not sinned, we make him a liar, and his word is not in us* (1 John 1:8–10).

While there may be some consequences we will have to work through, there is forgiveness from the Lord. He loves us. He will fight with us and for us. His instructions will show us how to triumph over our own mistakes and how to restore the broken areas.

The Lord did so with Israel when an enemy they were supposed to destroy deceived the nation. The Lord gave the Israelites battle instructions prior to entering the Promised Land. They were to clear the land of heathen nations according to the Lord's strategy and timing.

In the early chapters of the Book of Joshua, we see that Israel had famous battle victories. Their leader, Joshua, was careful to seek the Lord's counsel. Then we get to Chapter 9.

The nation Gibeon—aware of Israel's victories in Jericho and Ai—developed a plan to deceive their way out of defeat (Joshua 9:1–5). The Gibeonites had several of their men disguise themselves as ambassadors who traveled from a far country to develop an alliance with Israel. As proof of their supposed long-distance travel, these "ambassadors" were dressed in old garments and shoes. They carried worn-out sacks and wine bottles. Their bread was dry and moldy.

When asked by Joshua to identify themselves, the ambassadors gave a spiritual answer that seemed to give honor to God and His people. They said they came to the Israelites "because of the name of the Lord thy God" (Josh. 9:9). These men went on to describe Israel's victorious moments from gaining freedom from Egypt to being winners of wars.

Joshua and his men accepted the ambassadors' moldy evidence and alliance proposal.

> *And the men took of their victuals, and asked not counsel at the mouth of the Lord. And Joshua made peace with them, and made a league with them, to let them live: and the princes of the congregation sware unto them* (Josh. 9:14–15).

Joshua learned the truth three days later, when Israel discovered that the Gibeonites were their neighbors (Josh. 9:16) and were on the Lord's battle list.

Israel's leaders missed a victory opportunity against an enemy God marked for defeat. The leaders fell for the enemy's words of flattery and deceit. They did not seek the counsel of the all-knowing God.

The situation caused contention within Israel, as the nation was displeased with the leaders' decisions and the consequences. However, the leaders initiated another solution for dealing with the Gibeonites.

> *And Joshua called for them, and he spake unto them, saying, "Wherefore have ye beguiled us, saying, We are very far from you; when ye dwell among us? Now therefore ye are cursed, and there shall none of you be freed from being bondmen, and hewers of wood and drawers of water for the house of my God"* (Josh. 9: 22–23).

Israel still had to endure the consequences of their sins involving the Gibeonites. However, a misstep with one enemy did not mean all was lost with the Lord. He stayed by Israel's side as the people continued to face other enemy nations.

The alliance with the Gibeonites meant their war became Israel's war, as detailed in Joshua 10. Kings of five enemy nations decided to fight against Gibeon, described as a "great city," "one of the royal cities," and "greater than Ai" (which Israel had already defeated). In addition, Gibeon's men "were mighty" (Josh. 10:2). The five kings feared both Israel and Gibeon and did not like the two nations' alliance. With war approaching, the Gibeonites called for Israel's assistance.

> *And the men of Gibeon sent unto Joshua to the camp to Gilgal, saying, "Slack not thy hand from thy servants; come up to us quickly, and save us, and help us: for all the kings of the Amorites that dwell in the mountains are gathered together against us." So Joshua ascended from Gilgal, he, and all the people of war with him, and all the mighty men of valour* (Josh. 10:6–7).

Joshua and his army had to fight and win victory on behalf of a nation the Lord had told them to destroy. That is a heavy consequence to handle. Some of us are dealing with similar consequences.

We could have had outright victory, but we did not obey the Lord's instructions. We must tolerate less-effective solutions, as we had already given our word or acted on our decisions. Furthermore, we are pouring our time, energy, finances, and other resources into winning battles on behalf of something the Lord told us not to buy, sign up for, or invest in. Some of our self-initiated alliances and relationships are costing us dearly.

Just as Israel's loved ones risked their lives to benefit Gibeon, several of our loved ones' lives are suffering consequences because our battle sins have allowed an enemy to linger. However, the Lord is greater than our mistakes.

From Sins to Wins

The Lord stepped in to help Israel triumph over the five war-hungry nations that gathered against Gibeon.

> *And the Lord said unto Joshua, "Fear them not: for I have delivered them into thine hand; there shall not a man of them stand before thee" … And the Lord discomfited them before Israel, and slew them with a great slaughter at Gibeon … the Lord cast down great stones from heaven upon them … they were more which died with hailstones than they whom the children of Israel slew with the sword (Josh. 10:8, 10, 11).*

During the battle, Joshua commanded the sun and the moon to stand still, and the Lord kept the celestial bodies at bay (Josh. 10:12).

> *And the sun stood still, and the moon stayed, until the people had avenged themselves upon their enemies … So the sun stood still in the midst of heaven, and hasted not to go down about a whole day. And there was no day like that before it or after it, that the Lord hearkened unto the voice of a man: for the Lord fought for Israel (Josh. 10:13, 14).*

The Lord heard and helped His people even while they were dealing with the consequences of their earlier battle sins. He had forgiven them and fought on their behalf.

The Lord is here to help us successfully cope with the consequences of our battle sins. We must repent and ask the Lord to help us overcome our enemies. He is committed to our victories. We must be committed to His strategics.

Let Us Pray and Repent of Our Battle Sins (from Ps. 38:1, 18–22)

O Lord, rebuke me not in thy wrath: neither chasten me in thy hot displeasure ... For I will declare mine iniquity; I will be sorry for my sin. But mine enemies are lively, and they are strong: and they that hate me wrongfully are multiplied.

They also that render evil for good are mine adversaries; because I follow the thing that good is. Forsake me not, O Lord: O my God, be not far from me. Make haste to help me, O Lord my salvation. Amen.

Now, Be Encouraged by the Lord's Forgiveness and Mercy (from Ps. 103:8–9, 11–12, 14)

The Lord is merciful and gracious, slow to anger, and plenteous in mercy. He will not always chide: neither will he keep his anger for ever ... For as the heaven is high above the earth, so great is his mercy toward them that fear him. As far as the east is from the west, so far hath he removed our transgressions from us ...For he knoweth our frame; he remembereth that we are dust.

Restoration Battle

The Lord will give us victory beyond our mistakes. We must march on and fight the next battle. This is the restoration battle, where we get back to the triumphant ways. This is the battle where we have extraordinary experiences with the Lord's strategies and power.

Consider the great victory the Lord gave Israel after its mistakes with the Gibeonites. Israel went on to take down five kings in one battle. The Lord saved Israel years of warfare. He can do the same for us. He has the strategies that will ensure victories in several areas of our lives in one battle.

This is not the time to go on a guilt trip. Battles are raging. We cannot be discouraged and think, "I blew it, so the Lord won't help me."

The Lord will not leave us facing our enemies alone and defenseless. He is providing the weapons, resources, and time we need to battle effectively. We must get into the Lord's presence and let Him touch us with His battle-winning instructions.

> *The Lord is a man of war: the Lord is his name … Thy right hand, O Lord, is become glorious in power: thy right hand, O Lord, hath dashed in pieces the enemy* (Ex. 15:3, 6).

> *He teacheth my hands to war, so that a bow of steel is broken by mine arms … I have pursued mine enemies, and overtaken them: neither did I turn again till they were consumed … For thou hast girded me with strength unto the battle: thou hast subdued under me those that rose up against me* (Ps. 18:34, 37, 39).

> *But thanks be to God, which giveth us the victory through our Lord Jesus Christ* (1 Cor. 15:57).

CHAPTER 19

Battle Instructions
Part II: The Word Versus the Letter

For ever, O Lord, thy word is settled in heaven (Ps. 119:89).

The grass withereth, the flower fadeth: but the word of our God shall stand for ever (Isa. 40:8).

In the beginning was the Word, and the Word was with God, and the Word was God (John 1:1).

What did the Lord say? When we receive troublesome messages, we must turn to the Lord, who is the Word. He is the answer to those messages.

Before we go further into this instruction, we need to make sure we are not the enemy with a letter, but rather we are on the Word's side. A case in point: a Pharisee named Saul knew he was right in his efforts to capture, imprison, and kill the early Christians. He approved of the unbelievers' fatal stoning of Stephen, a deacon (Acts 8:1).

And Saul, yet breathing out threatenings and slaughter against the disciples of the Lord, went unto the high priest, And desired of him letters to Damascus to the synagogues, that if he found any of this way, whether they were men or women, he might bring them bound unto Jerusalem (Acts 9:1–2).

With permission letters in his hand, Saul was on his way to Damascus. He was determined to find more Christians to persecute for their belief in Jesus Christ—the Word made flesh to save humanity from sin. However, the letter-carrying Saul had an encounter with the Word:

> *And as he journeyed, he came near Damascus: and suddenly there shined round about him a light from heaven: And he fell to the earth, and heard a voice saying unto him, "Saul, Saul, why persecutest thou me?" And he said, "Who art thou, Lord?" And the Lord said, "I am Jesus whom thou persecutest: it is hard for thee to kick against the pricks"* (Acts 9:3–5).

After hearing from the Word, Saul acknowledged his need for salvation. Jesus sent Saul to receive instructions from a disciple named Ananias. Saul's life and name changed. He became the apostle Paul. Because of the Word, the letter-carrying persecutor became a letter-writing preacher spreading the Gospel of God.

Write Right

When the Lord stopped Saul on the road to Damascus, Christians were spared from being persecuted by him.

Though we have no intention to persecute others, some of us still need to be stopped from writing, mailing, e-mailing, or delivering letters that will indeed hurt the recipients. While we may think our messages are right, we need the Lord to show us whether we are on the Word side of these letter situations.

What did the Lord say? Are we in the right spiritual place to receive instruction concerning these letters? Are we writing God-directed words in those letters, whether they be business, legal, or personal? Will we have a testimony like Saul that by the time we got to the people we had letters for, we were the ones changed, instructed, and speaking the Lord's words?

None of us wants to be the enemy in situations where the Word battles letters. Those letters will not win, and the enemy suffers terrible consequences.

Consider Haman, a Persian government official in King Ahasuerus's court. Haman caused a tragic ending for himself and his family while losing a letter battle against God's people, as told in the Book of Esther.

Haman wanted all the Jews throughout the kingdom destroyed. He detailed his evil plans in letters he distributed to officials. He ordered them to organize deadly attacks against the Jews (Est. 3). However, the Lord worked through Queen Esther, the Jewish wife of King Ahasuerus, and through her cousin, Mordecai, to reverse Haman's plans.

The Jews received letters from Esther and Mordecai—with the king's authorization—instructing them to fight against their enemies on the day Haman had set for their destruction (Est. 8:7–17). The Jews followed their battle instructions and defeated their enemies. Haman's evil plot backfired. Actually, the king had Haman executed before the battling began (Est. 7:10). After their triumph, the Jews received another set of letters from Esther and Mordecai, instructing them to commemorate their victory with an annual celebration known today as Purim (Est. 9:20–32).

While we do not have Haman-like intentions to destroy people, we must be certain that we are not sending troubling messages that crush people's hopes and dreams or cause their relationships and friendships to crumble. We must make sure our correspondences do not cause disturbances to situations that can be resolved peacefully. We also must be sure that we are not sending forth messages, petitions, and legal documents in efforts to stop works that God has called to go forth.

Some Christians are heavily involved in local issues and start letter-writing campaigns in response to municipal plans and decisions. Their writing efforts start out with genuine concerns about the issues at hand. However, these writers' tones change when issues are not being resolved to their satisfaction. Their letters become personal, as they use angry and accusatory words against specific municipal officials. Some of these writers petition for officials' removal, though there are no ethical or legal reasons for such actions.

Some of these writers even dare to use the names of God and Jesus to justify their rants. These letter writers want the Lord to change municipal officials and issues. They do not realize that His first response will be to address their sinful letter-writing ways. Some people ignore the Lord's commands not to write or send letters.

When we engage in letter-writing projects, we should follow the example of prophets and apostles who wrote as God inspired them. Every word had purpose and conveyed the will of God.

The Lord knows how to write letters. We need Him to lead us in that process. He can show us the right words, phrases, and tones to use. We will benefit greatly from developing the habit of presenting our letters to the Lord for His review. He is the Word, who knows whether we are following our emotions or His will. He knows our letter-writing motives.

> *For the word of God is quick, and powerful, and sharper than any twoedged sword, piercing even to the dividing asunder of soul and spirit, and of the joints and marrow, and is a discerner of the thoughts and intents of the heart* (Heb. 4:12).

Taking Our Letters to The Word

Now that we have received instruction to be aware of our own correspondence conduct, we can go further into our lesson of how the Lord helps us overcome enemy-letter situations.

In Isaiah 36 and 37, we see how King Hezekiah, Judah's leader, turned to the Lord after receiving threats and an evil letter from Sennacherib, king of Assyria. The Assyrian king threatened to destroy Jerusalem and sent an army along as proof. He even lied through his messengers that God told him to destroy Judah. King Hezekiah took this issue straight to God.

> *And it came to pass, when king Hezekiah heard it, that he rent his clothes, and covered himself with sackcloth, and went into the house of the Lord* (Isa. 37:1).

Prior to this, Hezekiah had told the people of Judah not to respond to Sennacherib's messengers (Isa. 36:21). By calling for such silence, Hezekiah was setting the atmosphere for strictly hearing from the Lord. The Word, not people's responses, would save Judah and destroy the enemy.

The king also sent his servants to the prophet Isaiah.

> *And Isaiah said unto them, "Thus shall ye say unto your master, Thus saith the Lord, Be not afraid of the words that thou hast heard, wherewith the servants of the king of Assyria have blasphemed me. Behold, I will send a blast upon him, and he shall hear a rumour, and return to his own land; and I will cause him to fall by the sword in his own land"* (Isa. 37:6–7).

Hezekiah also took Sennecherib's threatening letter to the house of the Lord. He spread the letter out in the Lord's presence and prayed.

> *"Incline thine ear, O Lord, and hear; open thine eyes, O Lord, and see: and hear all the words of Sennacherib, which hath sent to reproach the living God … Now therefore, O Lord our God, save us from his hand, that all the kingdoms of the earth may know that thou art the Lord, even thou only"* (Isa. 37:17, 20).

Like Hezekiah, we can spread our letters in the presence of the Lord. We can let our tears fall before Him and be honest about our anger, frustrations, fears, and other emotions. Then we can have our minds, hearts, and bodies refreshed in His responses and instructions.

Hindering Letters Stopped by the Will of the Word

Judah was at a rebuilding moment in its history. The Lord had allowed Babylon to conquer Judah and destroy the temple because of Judah's refusals to repent of idolatry and other sins. However, Judah's temple rebuilding project was harassed, hindered, and halted by way of their enemies' letter-writing campaigns. In the end, the word of the Lord reigned, and the project was completed.

Let us review and learn from this situation.

When the rebuilding time had come, Persia was in power, having defeated Babylon. Cyrus, king of Persia, wrote a decree explaining that the Lord told him to have the Jerusalem temple rebuilt:

> *Now in the first year of Cyrus king of Persia, that the word of the Lord by the mouth of Jeremiah might be fulfilled, the*

Lord stirred up the spirit of Cyrus king of Persia, that he made a proclamation throughout all his kingdom, and put it also in writing, saying, "Thus saith Cyrus king of Persia, The Lord God of heaven hath given me all the kingdoms of the earth; and he hath charged me to build him an house at Jerusalem, which is in Judah" (Ezra 1:1–2).

When Cyrus asked who would return to Jerusalem to rebuild the temple, a portion of the captives taken from Judah during Babylon's reign volunteered to return for the project (Ezra 1:5). Cyrus gave them various items to help with the rebuilding effort. He also returned the vessels, basins, and other objects Babylon had taken from the original temple (Ezra 1:6–11).

After the rebuilding started, enemies of the project slowed its progress, as they did not want to see the temple or Jerusalem rebuilt (Ezra 4:1–4). These enemies were officials from other nations that had settled in nearby Israel (the Northern Kingdom) after its fall to Assyria, which occurred years before the downfall of Judah (the Southern Kingdom).

These enemies were able to get Judah's work halted completely by sending a letter to the Persian king Artaxerxes, who reigned after Cyrus. In the letter, the enemies falsely accused the people of Judah of doing more than rebuilding the temple. These letter-writers said the people were trying to rebuild Jerusalem, "the rebellious and the bad city," which would mean trouble for the Persian kingdom (Ezra 4:11–14). The enemies urged Artaxerxes to search through past rulers' record books to verify their Jerusalem-is-trouble claims (Ezra 4:15).

Artaxerxes did so and found writings about Jerusalem's "insurrection," "rebellion," and "sedition" against past kings (Ezra 4:19). He also learned that Jerusalem had a history of "mighty kings," who ruled other countries and had "toll, tribute and custom" paid to them (Ezra 4:20).

Not wanting this history repeated, Artaxerxes sent a letter to Jerusalem ordering the rebuilding project to stop. The work remained undone for more than fifteen years. However, the Lord stirred His people to start building again by sending prophets Haggai and Zechariah to speak to them and help them.

Then another group of enemies wrote a letter in attempts to stop the work again. This time, the enemies' letter went to the Persian king Darius. They wanted Darius to verify whether Judah's leaders were telling the truth about having permission from King Cyrus to rebuild the temple.

While Darius considered the contents of the letter, the people of Judah continued building, according to the will of God. Darius found Cyrus's decree that permitted the project and sent this response to Judah's enemies:

> "Now therefore, Tatnai, governor beyond the river, Shetharboznai, and your companions the Apharsachites, which are beyond the river, be ye far from thence: let the work of this house of God alone; let the governor of the Jews and the elders of the Jews build this house of God in his place" (Ezra 6:6–7).

Darius also told the enemies to give food and supplies that would make work and worship easier for the people of Judah (Ezra 6:8–12).

Before we move on to the next phase of our letter-battle instructions, we must review some issues concerning Judah's sinful past and how the enemies tried to use it.

While dealing with the second round of letter attacks, Judah's leaders acknowledged to their enemies that the nation's sins brought on the wrath of God, resulting in defeat to Babylon. However, Judah's leaders also identified themselves and their people as the servants of God, obeying His rebuilding commands (Ezra 5:11–12).

The leaders knew the Lord had forgiven their nation's past failures and was on their side. The Lord had given the prophet Zechariah a vision to encourage the people. In the vision, Satan accused Joshua, the high priest, of sin (Zech. 3:1–10). The Lord rebuked the accuser and restored Joshua. In this vision, Joshua represented the people of Judah. Though Satan continued to accuse, accuse, accuse, the Lord was moving His people from chastisement to restoration and rebuilding.

The Lord's vision and words withstood letters, records, and intimidation tactics used by enemies of His promise. The enemies pushed their own words about Judah. However, the Lord had already foretold His people's history.

The Lord revealed through the prophet Isaiah that Judah would be conquered because of its sins, His temple would be destroyed, and a ruler named Cyrus would see to its rebuilding (Isa. 44:28). Through

Jeremiah, the Lord said that Jerusalem would fall to Babylon and His people would be in exile for seventy years (Jer. 25:11–12). He later revealed through Daniel that Babylon would be destroyed by Persia as punishment for its wicked ways (Dan. 5:22–28).

The Lord knew enemies would hinder His people with letters and historical documents, so He inspired Cyrus to put in writing a decree allowing the rebuilding of the temple. Decades later, Cyrus's God-inspired words were still on record. Darius had to obey them, ordering the enemies to leave the work of the Lord alone.

Judah's experience shows us that a word from the Lord revealed in the past is more powerful than the enemy's attack in the present.

Some of us are going through repeated attacks in certain areas of our lives. We are flabbergasted and close to throwing up our hands in defeat as we frustratedly respond: "What now?" "Not again!" or "Oh, come on. Another letter?" Our frustration increases as we learn that our enemies are lying about our efforts and motives, while challenging our right to do the Lord's work. The enemies even point out our flaws and past shortcomings in efforts to disqualify us from our godly missions.

Are we so focused on our enemies' current attacks that we have forgotten—or not realized—that the prophecies, promises, and revelations the Lord gave us years ago are for our battles right now? No matter how many letters pop up, the Lord's words will prevail. So, have faith in God. He answered those letters before they were written.

> *"Remember the former things of old: for I am God, and there is none else; I am God, and there is none like me, Declaring the end from the beginning, and from ancient times the things that are not yet done, saying, 'My counsel shall stand, and I will do all my pleasure'"* (Isa. 46:9–10).

More Threats from the Enemy, More Words from the Lord

Judah encountered yet another letter battle almost seventy years after the temple's completion. This time, enemies waged a word-war against Jerusalem's efforts to reconstruct its broken-down walls and burned-up gates.

God used Nehemiah to lead the project. At the time, Judah was still in captivity, and Nehemiah was a cupbearer for the Persian ruler Artaxerxes. Nehemiah mourned for Jerusalem, Judah's capitol, after hearing about the condition of the city and the people's safety and quality-of-life issues (Neh. 1). He asked the king for permission to rebuild Jerusalem (Neh. 2). Nehemiah also asked Artaxerxes for letters authorizing travel protection and the acquisition of timber needed for the rebuilding project (Neh. 2:7).

With his requests granted, the letter-carrying Nehemiah traveled to Judah. After the reconstruction project began, enemies launched a letter-writing campaign against Nehemiah and the builders.

One letter—which Judah's enemies threatened to send to Artaxerxes—falsely claimed that Judah planned to rebel against Persia and that Nehemiah appointed prophets to preach that he was Judah's king. Nehemiah said he received other letters from his enemies bent on putting him and the people of Judah in fear.

Also announced against Nehemiah was a false prophecy about a plot to kill him (Neh. 6:10–12). However, Nehemiah kept the building project going, refusing to come down from the wall. He had asked God to strengthen his hands (Neh. 6:9), so he and the builders would not become weak with fear. They needed to be strong physically, spiritually, and emotionally so they could complete their task.

The Lord answered their prayers, and they finished the wall. Even their defeated enemies had to admit the building project was the Lord's doing (Neh. 6:15–16).

Like Nehemiah, we cannot get discouraged or distracted by Satan's tactics designed to undermine the restorative work the Lord is doing in and through us. No matter what the enemy writes, the Lord is the author and finisher of our faith (Heb. 12:2). The powerful word of the Lord protects us and crushes the enemy's declarations.

> "Is not my word like as a fire?" saith the Lord; "and like a hammer that breaketh the rock in pieces?" (Jer. 23:29).

The Word Has the Last Say

There are times when the enemy does execute plans outlined in letters written against God's people. To several of us, God seems to be absent in those letter situations because He does not prevent the enemy's plans from happening. As a result, we suffer losses and we're stunned.

However, we must trust that the Lord will not leave us to suffer utter defeat at the hands of the enemy. The Lord will handle our letter issues. He will avenge us.

> *The righteous shall rejoice when he seeth the vengeance ... So that a man shall say, Verily there is a reward for the righteous: verily he is a God that judgeth in the earth* (Ps. 58:10–11).

> *"And shall not God avenge his own elect, which cry day and night unto him, though he bear long with them?"* (Luke 18:7).

Let us consider Naboth, a godly man who lost his life and his land in a letter situation (1 Kings 21). However, the Lord avenged Naboth's death and used the land in judgment against those who took it.

Full of wickedness and greed, King Ahab wanted to purchase Naboth's vineyard, situated near the palace. However, Naboth refused Ahab's offer. Naboth chose to obey the Lord's law that forbade the sale of inherited land (1 Kings 21:1–3).

The seething Ahab returned to his palace, where his wife, Jezebel, learned about the vineyard situation. She promised Ahab that she would give him Naboth's vineyard (verse 7).

Jezebel wrote a letter in Ahab's name to elders and nobles living near Naboth. She told them to find two witnesses who would falsely accuse Naboth of blaspheming God and the king. As a result, Naboth was stoned and Ahab took the land (verses 8–16).

Though Jezebel's evil letter plan seemed successful, the Lord had the final say concerning the situation. Through the prophet Elijah, the Lord pronounced death for Ahab and Jezebel (1 Kings 21:20–24). Later, their wicked son, King Jehoram, was killed and buried in the vineyard (2 Kings 9:24–26).

Naboth lost his earthly life, but he has eternal life with the Lord and a greater vineyard and reward in God's kingdom. Naboth's memory—and the Lord's vengeance on his behalf—are permanently part of God's Word.

While we may not understand why certain things happen, we must believe that the Word is with us and never loses. Though letter trials arise from the enemy, the Word will stand up for us and eradicate the enemy's plans. The Word will have the last say.

> *The LORD bringeth the counsel of the heathen to nought: he maketh the devices of the people of none effect. The counsel of the LORD standeth for ever, the thoughts of his heart to all generations* (Ps. 33:10–11).

> *There are many devices in a man's heart; nevertheless the counsel of the LORD, that shall stand* (Prov. 19:21).

> *Take counsel together, and it shall come to nought; speak the word, and it shall not stand: for God is with us* (Isaiah 8:10).

CHAPTER 20

Battle Instructions
Part III: Outnumbered But Not Overpowered

The Lord is my light and my salvation; whom shall I fear? the Lord is the strength of my life; of whom shall I be afraid? When the wicked, even mine enemies and my foes, came upon me to eat up my flesh, they stumbled and fell. Though an host should encamp against me, my heart shall not fear: though war should rise against me, in this will I be confident (Ps. 27:1–3).

While facing a multitude of enemies in our battle situations, we overcome fear and weakness by relying on the Lord to be our light, salvation, and strength. His strategy does not fall apart when we are outnumbered.

While preparing to enter Canaan, the people of Israel received instructions to clear out the enemy nations in order to take possession of their Promised Land.

When the Lord thy God shall bring thee into the land whither thou goest to possess it, and hath cast out many nations before thee, the Hittites, and the Girgashites, and the Amorites, and the Canaanites, and the Perizzites, and the Hivites, and the Jebusites, seven nations greater and mightier than thou (Deut. 7:1).

That was quite a to-do list. However, the long list of enemies represented a long list of victories God had in store for Israel. The Lord knew His people were outnumbered, but he still assigned them the Promised Land because of His love and His promise.

> *The Lord did not set his love upon you, nor choose you, because ye were more in number than any people; for ye were the fewest of all people: But because the Lord loved you, and because he would keep the oath which he had sworn unto your fathers, hath the Lord brought you out with a mighty hand, and redeemed you out of the house of bondmen, from the hand of Pharaoh king of Egypt* (Deut. 7:7–8).

In Judges 6 and 7, the Lord revealed battle duties to Gideon. The Lord's strategy called for Gideon's army to be outnumbered by its enemies, the Midianites. The Lord did not want Gideon and his army to become boastful and take the credit for their victory.

> *And the Lord said unto Gideon, "The people that are with thee are too many for me to give the Midianites into their hands, lest Israel vaunt themselves against me, saying, 'Mine own hand hath saved me'"* (Judg. 7:2).

Gideon's army shrank from thirty-two thousand to three hundred as the Lord set the standard of who would battle. Dismissed from battle were those who were "fearful and afraid" (Judg. 7:3) and those who did not scoop up water with their hands to drink it (Judg. 7:4–7).

As we face our battles, we should seek the Lord's standards as to who is to be involved. He may dismiss people from our situations. Some of us are hurt because certain friends, relatives, and church members were not by our side in the heat of our battles. Have we considered that they did not fit into the Lord's strategy concerning our victories?

The Lord knows who will try to take over or take credit, who lacks the faith needed to endure the circumstances, and who is not in the right spiritual position or emotional condition to overcome the enemies' tactics. The Lord also knows who will obey His battle instructions no matter how strange the strategy or weaponry.

Gideon needed soldiers who were willing to fight; the Lord wanted soldiers who would obey. When the time came for battle, the three hundred soldiers carried trumpets and pitchers containing lighted torches to their assigned battle positions. These soldiers had to follow Gideon's orders precisely.

> *And he said unto them, "Look on me, and do likewise: and, behold, when I come to the outside of the camp, it shall be that, as I do, so shall ye do. When I blow with a trumpet, I and all that are with me, then blow ye the trumpets also on every side of all the camp, and say, The sword of the Lord, and of Gideon"* (Judg. 7:17–18).

As the soldiers obeyed, the Lord caused confusion in the enemy's camp. The Midianites began to kill one another (Judg. 7:20–23). Those who survived ran away. However, Gideon sent word that other Hebrew tribes in the region were to war against the fleeing Midianites (Judg. 7:24–25). The enemy was thoroughly defeated, as the Lord had promised.

When facing multitudes of enemies, "Lord, help us" is a great battle cry that causes us to shift our focus from our adversaries and to our Lord.

> *Plead my cause, O Lord, with them that strive with me: fight against them that fight against me. Take hold of shield and buckler, and stand up for mine help* (Ps. 35:1–2).

King Jehoshaphat and the people of Judah called on the Lord for help after learning that three enemy nations banded together to wage war against them.

> *And Jehoshaphat feared, and set himself to seek the Lord, and proclaimed a fast throughout all Judah. And Judah gathered themselves together, to ask help of the Lord: even out of all the cities of Judah they came to seek the Lord* (2 Chron. 20:3–4).

Speaking through the prophet Jahaziel, the Lord answered their cry with encouragement and promise of victory. He reassured them that He had ownership of the battle (2 Chron. 20:15). The Lord also announced

His strategy as He revealed where the enemies would position themselves on battle day. He told Judah when and where to advance. Then He told them what they would not be doing in the war:

> *"Ye shall not need to fight in this battle: set yourselves, stand ye still, and see the salvation of the Lord with you, O Judah and Jerusalem: fear not, nor be dismayed; to morrow go out against them: for the Lord will be with you"* (2 Chron. 20:17).

Judah's soldiers would have to stay where the Lord strategically placed them. Though Judah had often engaged in warfare, this battle would not require traditional fighting from its soldiers. Having received the Lord's battle instructions, King Jehoshaphat placed his people in proper victory position, sending out the singers before the soldiers.

> *And when he had consulted with the people, he appointed singers unto the Lord, and that should praise the beauty of holiness, as they went out before the army, and to say, "Praise the Lord; for his mercy endureth for ever." And when they began to sing and to praise, the Lord set ambushments against the children of Ammon, Moab, and mount Seir, which were come against Judah; and they were smitten* (2 Chron. 20:21–22).

Judah's relationship with the Lord determined its reactions to the enemies' battle plans. To win the battle, Judah did everything "unto the Lord" (2 Chron. 20:21), from crying out for help to worshipping on the battlefield.

When battle arises, we—like Judah—should go into "unto the Lord" mode, staying focused on His presence, while seeking, trusting, and obeying His strategies. Then we will increase in faith enough to release a war cry of worship while the Lord goes before us, wreaking havoc on the enemy. To be battle strong, we must be relationship strong with our Lord. Relationship with the Lord is more powerful than any battle the enemy dares to wage.

I will love thee, O Lord, my strength ... I will call upon the Lord, who is worthy to be praised: so shall I be saved from mine enemies (Ps. 18:1, 3).

He delivered me from my strong enemy, and from them which hated me: for they were too strong for me ... He brought me forth also into a large place; he delivered me, because he delighted in me (Ps. 18:17, 19).

For the eyes of the Lord run to and fro throughout the whole earth, to shew himself strong in the behalf of them whose heart is perfect toward him (2 Chron. 16:9).

The early Church remained intact despite much scattering due to persecution. The Church grew as scattered Christians stayed faithful in their relationship with the Lord and obeyed His instructions to spread the Gospel.

The enemies of life—including death—do not have the power to destroy our relationship with the Lord. This love relationship is forever. No enemy can conquer it, and no war can wear it down.

Who shall separate us from the love of Christ? shall tribulation, or distress, or persecution, or famine, or nakedness, or peril, or sword? As it is written, For thy sake we are killed all the day long; we are accounted as sheep for the slaughter. Nay, in all these things we are more than conquerors through him that loved us (Rom. 8:35–37).

Outnumbered While Protecting the Productive Place

The field was full of barley ready for Judah's use. However, their enemies, the Philistines, threatened to take possession of the field, meaning the people of Judah would be without food. The productive place was left vulnerable and almost empty after Judah's army ran from the Philistines (1 Chron. 11:12–14; 2 Sam. 23:9–10). However, Eleazar, one of King David's mightiest warriors, stayed on the field, fighting past the point of his own weariness.

He arose, and smote the Philistines until his hand was weary, and his hand clave unto the sword: and the Lord wrought a great victory that day; and the people returned after him only to spoil (2 Sam. 23:10).

Through this barley-field battle, the Lord reminds us that Satan and his cohorts will go after our productive places, those areas where we are maturing, completing assignments for the Lord, and influencing others to live for Christ. Satan is attracted to productive places because he wants to have power over them and use them for his own vile activities, while keeping people from receiving the benefits of these places. The devil wants to take over Bible studies, youth groups, and church councils and consistories. He wants to drain households, marriages, finances, and Christian-based agencies set up to help people in need.

Satan's battle tactics are not new. When he was an angel named Lucifer, Satan started a war in heaven, wanting to take God's throne in the very place where praise and worship originated. God and His mighty host threw Lucifer and his fellow revolting angels out of heaven.

The Lord wants to help us to protect the productive places and kick Satan out. The key is to remain fully focused on our mission and dependent on the Lord.

Forgiveness for Fleeing Warriors

Eleazar's supposed battle buddies retreated when the enemy army advanced. However, they returned after the battle to collect their dead enemies' valuables.

Oftentimes, the Lord will use us to manifest great victories that benefit those who did not stand with us in battle. They did not intend to abandon us, but they were too afraid of the enemy to stick around. We must thank God for His victory and forgive those who ran away. We must also ask the Lord to strengthen and bless them as they continue the process of growing into fearless warriors for Him.

Some of us have been fearful runners. We can repent to the Lord and continue to mature in faith. If possible, we should express our apologies to the warriors we abandoned and learn how we can assist them as they continue to protect the productive places. Several of us need to return to prayer groups, church committees, community organizations, friendships, and family members, not to collect the valuables, but to thank them for staying in the fight after we ran away.

In 2 Timothy 2:3, we are instructed to endure hardness as good soldiers of Jesus Christ. There must be a determination within us that we will not run away from the challenges that are part of living this Christian life, nor quit the work the Lord has given us because of a field full of enemies. Like Eleazar, we have to be willing to endure hardness in the heat of the battle. His experience shows us the determination and knowledge required to stay on the field and overcome the enemies of our productive places.

There are three points to note concerning the battle actions of Eleazar.

Point One: Eleazar Was Aware of the Product and Value of the Field

He knew that the field, which was full of barley, was worth the fight. He knew that if the Philistines got the field, they would gain territory and have food to strengthen them for more battle. On the other hand, Judah would starve, making them an easy target for defeat.

How much do we value our productive places? Does the enemy know the value of our productive places more than we do? What kind of battle advantages would our enemies gain if they got hold of our productive places?

Point Two: Eleazar Struck Down the Philistines

In 2 Samuel 23:9, we see that "he arose," meaning that Eleazar was up for the challenge and had gone on the offensive. In this warrior's mind, the Philistines were not getting that field. The warrior engaged in the type of action that brought down the enemy. He was skilled on how to use weaponry and where to strike fatal blows. As a warrior in David's army, Eleazar faced the Philistines many times and knew their fighting style. He also had to know evasive moves that kept the enemies from fatally striking him.

We need the Lord to train us to become skilled warriors in the spiritual warfare against Satan and his army. We need instructions on how to strike the enemy, disable his weapons, and render his plans and activities ineffective.

*He teacheth my hands to war, so that a bow of steel is
broken by mine arms ... For thou hast girded me with
strength unto the battle: thou hast subdued under me those
that rose up against me (Ps. 18:34, 39).*

*Blessed be the Lord my strength which teacheth my hands
to war, and my fingers to fight (Ps. 144:1).*

*Finally, my brethren, be strong in the Lord, and in the
power of his might. Put on the whole armour of God, that
ye may be able to stand against the wiles of the devil ...
above all, taking the shield of faith, wherewith ye shall
be able to quench all the fiery darts of the wicked (Eph.
6:10–11, 16).*

Point Three: Eleazar Kept Swinging

Eleazar fought so much and so hard his hand became weary and
"clave unto the sword" (2 Sam. 23:10). The committed warrior fought
beyond his weariness. The battle was beyond him. At some point,
Eleazar's hand became frozen to the sword. He and the weapon moved
as one unit. This warrior could not let go of the sword if he wanted to.
The focus was no longer on holding the sword, but keeping it in motion.
The weary warrior kept swinging.

Eleazar's hand is symbolic of our lives, while the sword represents
the Word of God (Eph. 6:17). We must become so committed to the
Lord and His productive places that we wrap our lives around His
Word. In times when we are beyond weary, we must remain frozen
to His Word, which helps us to continue functioning. As we saw with
Eleazar, the enemies that surround us will be defeated on every side.

The place where Eleazar and the Philistines fought was called Pasdammim (1 Chron. 11:13), which means "place of bloodshed."[5] Eleazar
means "God has helped."[6] Therefore, we have this testimony: God has
helped in a place of bloodshed. Because of the battle, the productive
place became a place of bloodshed, the evidence of the enemy's defeat.

We, too, must persevere through our places of bloodshed. These are
places of tears, frustration, and sacrifice; places where those who were

supposed to fight with us abandoned us; and places where we battle beyond our mental, physical, and emotional weariness.

This is the battlefield where enemies are advancing from every angle. We take down one enemy. Here comes another. We are enduring through situation after situation, heartache after heartache, and pain after pain. However, the Lord will deliver and deliver and deliver.

> *Many are the afflictions of the righteous: but the Lord delivereth him out of them all* (Ps. 34:19).

The places where enemies war against us are the places where the Lord will give us great deliverances (1 Chron. 11:14) and great victories (2 Sam. 23:10). Just hold onto the sword and keep swinging. Don't give up on the productive places. The mighty, victorious move of God is there. So, keep preaching. Keep praying. Keep singing. Keep praising. Keep worshiping. Keep serving. Keep giving. Keep believing. Keep obeying. Just keep swinging. The Lord will put the yoke-destroying, enemy-defeating power in the swing.

Meditate upon this message from the Lord, pieced together from examples and words of 1 Chron. 11:12–14 and 2 Sam. 23:9–10.

"I am the power of the ministry, the strength of your efforts. Just stay in the productive place, in the field where I placed you. I'll keep you standing, and I'll keep you swinging. You can't let go of your weapon. You can't put it down because I won't let you.

"You are connected to My Word. You are connected to what I gave you to defend—the productive place. I will keep you vigilant and victorious. I'll keep you strong. And I'm going to keep you right there fighting to protect the productive place until the defeat of the enemy is manifested."

CHAPTER 21

Battle Instructions
Part IV: Final Victory

Jesus looked like a loser on that cross. He was beaten, whipped, spit on, and nailed. The water-walking miracle worker—who raised the dead, healed those who touched Him, multiplied food to feed thousands, and called Himself the Messiah—was hanging bloody on a cross. The Eternal Victorious One looked like a beaten-down, defeated, dying man too weak to help himself. The Son of God, who powerfully taught and preached to multitudes, looked too weak to counter the words of His mockers.

> *Likewise also the chief priests mocking him, with the scribes and elders, said, "He saved others; himself he cannot save. If he be the King of Israel, let him now come down from the cross, and we will believe him. He trusted in God; let him deliver him now, if he will have him: for he said, 'I am the Son of God'"* (Matt. 27:41–43).

> *And they that passed by railed on him, wagging their heads, and saying, "Ah, thou that destroyest the temple, and buildest it in three days, Save thyself, and come down from the cross." Likewise also the chief priests mocking said among themselves with the scribes, "He saved others; himself he cannot save. Let Christ the King of Israel descend now from the cross, that we may see and believe." And they that were crucified with him reviled him"* (Mark 15:29–32).

> *And the people stood beholding. And the rulers also with them derided him, saying, "He saved others; let him save himself, if he be Christ, the chosen of God." And the soldiers also mocked him, coming to him, and offering him vinegar, And saying, "If thou be the king of the Jews, save thyself"* (Luke 23:35–37).

However, dying on the cross was Christ's great victorious moment. He paid humanity's penalty for sin, opening the way for us to be reconciled with God. Though this moment did not look, sound, or feel good, Jesus knew the glory and the salvation that would result from Him successfully dying on the cross.

> *For God so loved the world, that he gave his only begotten Son, that whosoever believeth in him should not perish, but have everlasting life. For God sent not his Son into the world to condemn the world; but that the world through him might be saved* (John 3:16–17).

> *And Jesus answered them, saying, "The hour is come, that the Son of man should be glorified ... Now is my soul troubled; and what shall I say? Father, save me from this hour: but for this cause came I unto this hour ... And I, if I be lifted up from the earth, will draw all men unto me." This he said, signifying what death he should die* (John 12:23, 27, 32–33).

> *Looking unto Jesus the author and finisher of our faith; who for the joy that was set before him endured the cross, despising the shame, and is set down at the right hand of the throne of God* (Heb. 12:2).

When We Look Like We Lost

Through His life and death experiences, Jesus showed us how to persevere when we look like the enemy has defeated us. He showed us how to continue living victoriously while suffering from the enemy's battle blows.

The Lord is calling for mature saints willing to remain faithful in those seasons where they look like they lost—the illness has not gone away, the bank account is still empty, and the church pews are almost bare. The Lord is our Victory, who knows how to bring triumphant results into our seemingly losing moments.

> *And we know that all things work together for good to them that love God, to them who are the called according to his purpose* (Rom. 8:28).

> *Blessed is the man that endureth temptation: for when he is tried, he shall receive the crown of life, which the Lord hath promised to them that love him* (James 1:12).

We dare not lose our eternal victory over a momentary look. Throughout the Bible, the Lord has shown us people who remained faithful as they endured afflictions and attacks of the enemy.

Joseph was thrown in prison. Daniel was thrown in the lion's den. Shadrach, Meshach, and Abednego were thrown into the fiery furnace. Jeremiah was thrown in a pit. They looked like they had lost. Yet they trusted in the Lord. As a result, the Lord prospered them.

Let us revisit the suffering of Job to learn about the ultimate victory he—and God—won against Satan.

Satan began his attacks after he challenged God that Job would curse God if Job lost his wealth. Though Job did not understand why he and his wife were going through such horrific experiences, he remained faithful in his relationship with the Lord. Notice Job's response to news that his children, servants, and animals were killed:

> *Then Job arose, and rent his mantle, and shaved his head, and fell down upon the ground, and worshipped, And said, "Naked came I out of my mother's womb, and naked shall I return thither: the Lord gave, and the Lord hath taken away; blessed be the name of the Lord." In all this Job sinned not, nor charged God foolishly* (Job 1:20–22).

Job lost almost everything, but he did not lose his capacity to be a blessing to God. Job was still spiritually wealthy enough to worship God and proclaim blessings for His name. That's victory!

Job endured a severe illness that caused his body to be covered with boils, which he scraped off with broken glass (Job 2). His grief-stricken wife offered ungodly advice on how he should deal with this situation. However, Job remained victoriously faithful to God.

> *Then said his wife unto him, "Dost thou still retain thine integrity? curse God, and die." But he said unto her, "Thou speakest as one of the foolish women speaketh. What? shall we receive good at the hand of God, and shall we not receive evil?" In all this did not Job sin with his lips* (Job 2:9–10).

Then Job's so-called friends blamed him for his sufferings, insisting that the Lord was punishing him for unrepented sins. Still, Job kept his focus on the Lord, seeking Him for understanding and trusting Him to bring good out of the horrible circumstances.

> *Behold, I go forward, but he is not there; and backward, but I cannot perceive him: On the left hand, where he doth work, but I cannot behold him: he hideth himself on the right hand, that I cannot see him: But he knoweth the way that I take: when he hath tried me, I shall come forth as gold. My foot hath held his steps, his way have I kept, and not declined* (Job 23:8–11).

At the end of Job's suffering period, God blessed him with more children and gave him double of all he had lost (Job 42:10–17).

The ultimate victory of Job's situation was in his refusal to curse God. Satan could not get Job to do that. The devil continues to experience defeat by faith-filled people's refusal to turn their backs on God and His words.

The Bible shows how the people of God were afflicted, beaten, ostracized, tormented, tortured, imprisoned, and killed, while holding onto the ultimate victory of knowing, loving, and trusting God (Heb. 11:32–40). They focused on the eternal victory of living forever with the Lord. They had faith in the Lord's victorious promise that if they suffered and died with Him, they shall live and reign with Him (2 Tim. 2:10–12); and they shall "be glad also with exceeding joy" when Christ's glory is revealed to the world (1 Peter 4:13).

The victory of the sufferings we endure in our battles is that Christ is glorified.

If ye be reproached for the name of Christ, happy are ye; for the spirit of glory and of God resteth upon you: on their part he is evil spoken of, but on your part he is glorified ... Yet if any man suffer as a Christian, let him not be ashamed; but let him glorify God on this behalf (1 Peter 4:14, 16).

For the apostle Paul, his losses and sufferings could not compare to the victory of being in an intimate relationship with Christ.

Yea doubtless, and I count all things but loss for the excellency of the knowledge of Christ Jesus my Lord: for whom I have suffered the loss of all things, and do count them but dung, that I may win Christ ... That I may know him, and the power of his resurrection, and the fellowship of his sufferings, being made conformable unto his death; If by any means I might attain unto the resurrection of the dead (Phil. 3:8, 10–11).

When the early Church appeared to be losing battles against persecutions, Paul reminded its members that their Savior had already sealed their final victory of being with Him.

For the Lord himself shall descend from heaven with a shout, with the voice of the archangel, and with the trump of God: and the dead in Christ shall rise first: Then we which are alive and remain shall be caught up together with them in the clouds, to meet the Lord in the air: and so shall we ever be with the Lord. Wherefore comfort one another with these words (1 Thess. 4:16–18).

Because we believe the testimony of Jesus' resurrection, we have faith that we, too, shall live forever in him. His resurrection proved to the world that death has no power over Him. In Jesus is victory over sin, triumph over death, and eternal life.

He will swallow up death in victory; and the Lord GOD will wipe away tears from off all faces; and the rebuke of his people shall he take away from off all the earth: for the Lord hath spoken it (Isa. 25:8).

*O death, where is thy sting? O grave, where is thy victory?…
But thanks be to God, which giveth us the victory through
our Lord Jesus Christ* (1 Cor. 15:55, 57).

Final Victory

While we war with the enemy daily, God holds our final victory in
His hands. He is not a weakling wondering what Satan is going to do
next. Our invincible Lord is the Glorious Victor of the ultimate battle
against every agent working on Satan's behalf.

Jesus—our Savior who endured the cross—is Lord, the Everlasting
Word of God. The Word is a fearless warrior charging into battle with
one result in mind—victory. He is not going to argue with Satan or
negotiate some kind of deal with this devil. The Word will cast Satan
into the lake of fire to burn and be in torment forever.

Through the Old Testament prophet Isaiah, the Lord spoke of His
final victory over His enemy.

> *In that day the Lord with his sore and great and strong
> sword shall punish leviathan the piercing serpent, even
> leviathan that crooked serpent; and he shall slay the dragon
> that is in the sea* (Isa. 27:1).

The New Testament apostle John writes that Satan is "the dragon,
that old serpent, which is the Devil" (Rev. 20:2). In Revelations 19 and
20, the Lord gave the apostle John visions and spiritual interactions in
His kingdom, revealing some details of the final victory the Word shall
win for us.

Let us rejoice in the Word as we read these victorious verses from
Revelations 19:

> *And I saw heaven opened, and behold a white horse; and
> he that sat upon him was called Faithful and True, and in
> righteousness he doth judge and make war* (verse 11).
>
> *And he was clothed with a vesture dipped in blood: and his
> name is called The Word of God* (verse 13).

And out of his mouth goeth a sharp sword, that with it he should smite the nations: and he shall rule them with a rod of iron: and he treadeth the winepress of the fierceness and wrath of Almighty God. And he hath on his vesture and on his thigh a name written, "KING OF KINGS, AND LORD OF LORDS" (verses 15–16).

And I saw the beast, and the kings of the earth, and their armies, gathered together to make war against him that sat on the horse, and against his army. And the beast was taken, and with him the false prophet that wrought miracles before him … These both were cast alive into a lake of fire burning with brimstone (verses 19, 20).

And the remnant were slain with the sword of him that sat upon the horse, which sword proceeded out of his mouth: and all the fowls were filled with their flesh (verse 21).

Our rejoicing continues as we read about the ultimate defeat of Satan:

And the devil that deceived them was cast into the lake of fire and brimstone, where the beast and the false prophet are, and shall be tormented day and night for ever and ever (Rev. 20:10).

Just like that, it's all over. The battle is done, the victory is won, and the enemy is gone.

While defeating Satan and his army, the Lord avenged the blood of apostles, prophets, and saints who endured sufferings, persecutions, and martyrdoms for His sake (Rev. 18:20, 19:2). The Lord kept His promise that He would indeed make the enemy pay for attacking and battling His people.

"To me belongeth vengeance and recompence; their foot shall slide in due time: for the day of their calamity is at hand, and the things that shall come upon them make haste" (Deut. 32:35).

> *Dearly beloved, avenge not yourselves, but rather give place unto wrath: for it is written, "Vengeance is mine; I will repay," saith the Lord* (Rom. 12:19).

When the enemy wages war against us, the Word charges in on our behalf. For every battle, the Word has the final say and the final act of victory. He knows the fate of our foe. Therefore, we must remain encouraged and confident in our Lord. We must be open to receiving His presence, touches, and guidance as He reveals how He will manifest Himself in our battles.

> *Lift up your heads, O ye gates; and be ye lift up, ye everlasting doors; and the King of glory shall come in. Who is this King of glory? The Lord strong and mighty, the Lord mighty in battle* (Ps. 24:7–8).

In John 16:33, Jesus told His disciples they would experience tribulation in the world. However, he instructed them to "be of good cheer" because he has overcome the world.

Let us glorify the Lord, who has done mighty acts on our behalf. Let us testify of His might and magnify Him above every enemy and situation we face. Rejoice! No one and nothing can overturn the Lord's victory. It's final and eternal.

> *Thine, O Lord is the greatness, and the power, and the glory, and the victory, and the majesty: for all that is in the heaven and in the earth is thine; thine is the kingdom, O Lord, and thou art exalted as head above all. Both riches and honour come of thee, and thou reignest over all; and in thine hand is power and might; and in thine hand it is to make great, and to give strength unto all. Now therefore, our God, we thank thee, and praise thy glorious name* (1 Chron. 29:11–13).

> *O sing unto the Lord a new song; for he hath done marvellous things: his right hand, and his holy arm, hath gotten him the victory* (Ps. 98:1).

CHAPTER 22

Touched with Intimacy
A Touching Relationship with the Lord

"Who touched Me?"

The crowd swarmed Jesus. People were pressing toward Him, reaching for Him, desperate for some kind of contact with Him. Then he felt the touch. Someone had gotten to Him.

> *And Jesus said, "Who touched me?" When all denied, Peter and they that were with him said, "Master, the multitude throng thee and press thee, and sayest thou, Who touched me?" And Jesus said, "Somebody hath touched me: for I perceive that virtue is gone out of me." And when the woman saw that she was not hid, she came trembling, and falling down before him, she declared unto him before all the people for what cause she had touched him, and how she was healed immediately. And he said unto her, "Daughter, be of good comfort: thy faith hath made thee whole; go in peace"* (Luke 8:45–48).

Jesus found the source and testimony of the touch. He faced the suffering woman. She had a medical issue that caused her to bleed continuously. She had touched the One who was sent to suffer, bleed, and die for the natural and spiritual healing of humankind. Her bleeding stopped.

The woman had only meant to make minimal contact with Jesus' robe. However, her touch came with faith, reverence, and instructions. Her touch went beyond His earthly garb and made contact with His divine identity, resulting in the outpouring of His power. The Word had received the touch and words of this woman and responded with power.

This touching exchange between Jesus and the woman shows us we can experience an outpouring of the power of God by touching Him. From this woman's experience, we learn the magnitude of being in the presence of the Lord with the intention of touching Him with words expressing our total dependence on Him. We touch the Lord by letting Him know that we cannot live without Him and He is the only One who brings salvation, healing, restoration, and wholeness to our lives.

Because of this woman's condition, she was not supposed to be where Jesus was, according to law and societal customs. She was not supposed to be around the people crowding Him. She was not supposed to be touching anyone. Yet she went beyond the law to touch Him who fulfilled the law. For this woman, Jesus meant more than "not supposed to be," so she put herself in the mental, emotional, spiritual, and physical positions needed to get close to Him. She crawled and stretched through the crowds of "not supposed to be" and touched Him who says all things are possible to them that believe (Mark 9:23).

Many people will tell us what we are not supposed to be, but Jesus knows who we are. The woman was a social outcast, only known by her condition. However, Jesus called her daughter. He loved her, and she belonged to Him. Their connection would go beyond that moment. Jesus showed that He would be committed to caring for her as a father continuously cares for his child. He declared her whole—restored to health and to the benefits, productivity, and responsibilities that come with receiving healing. Jesus also told the woman to be of good comfort and to go on with her life in peace. All of these wonderful things happened to her because she touched Him.

While on earth, Jesus knew that crowds of people would reach for Him as He traveled to preach the Gospel. Nevertheless, He walked among them, making Himself available and reachable for touch. Many people were "made perfectly whole" as they touched Jesus' garments (Matt. 14:34–36).

Intimately Touching the Lord

Many people were in the room, but the woman only saw Jesus. She headed straight for Jesus. She poured expensive oil on his head and feet. She washed his feet with her tears. She kissed his feet and wiped them with her hair.

People in the room criticized the woman. Jesus defended her.

> *And Jesus said, "Let her alone; why trouble ye her? she hath wrought a good work on me ... She hath done what she could: she is come aforehand to anoint my body to the burying. Verily I say unto you, Wheresoever this gospel shall be preached throughout the whole world, this also that she hath done shall be spoken of for a memorial of her"* (Mark 14:6, 8–9).

John 11:1–2 identifies the woman as Mary, the sister of Martha and of Lazarus, whom Jesus raised from the dead. Mary's worship with tears and expensive ointment had blessed Jesus, physically and spiritually. She anointed the Anointed One. She freely poured out her adoration, giving her all to the One who would give His all to save all from all sin and all diseases.

Jesus made sure none would forget her all-inspiring worship, a worship that would inspire others to surrender their all to the all-knowing, all-present, and all-powerful God.

Mary's worship time with Jesus should encourage us to do more than seek an outpouring experience from the Lord. We also should render Him outpourings of love, submission, thankfulness, tenderness, and tears. Mary even involved her hair in the worship experience, showing us that every fiber of our being is to be humbled and bowed down before Him.

> *O come, let us worship and bow down: let us kneel before the Lord our maker* (Ps. 95:6).

> *Exalt ye the Lord our God, and worship at his footstool; for he is holy* (Ps. 99:5).

> *We will go into his tabernacles: we will worship at his footstool* (Ps. 132:7).

As He did with Mary, the Lord will protect the intimate relationship we have with Him. He will tell the enemies of worship to leave us alone. He will not let critics keep us from touching Him.

Jesus is so committed to having an intimate, touching relationship with us that He allowed Himself to be touched with torment to pay the ultimate price for our sins. He allowed fists, whips, thorns, nails, a cross, a sword, and death to touch Him for our salvation.

> *But he was wounded for our transgressions, he was bruised for our iniquities: the chastisement of our peace was upon him; and with his stripes we are healed* (Isa. 53:5).

> *But God commendeth his love toward us, in that, while we were yet sinners, Christ died for us* (Rom. 5:8).

Touched Beyond Doubt

While meeting with His disciples after His death and resurrection, Jesus showed them His nail-scarred hands. He also let them see the evidence of being pierced in his side (John 20:19–20). The disciple Thomas was not at the meeting and refused to believe the other disciples' testimonies about seeing Jesus.

> *The other disciples therefore said unto him, "We have seen the Lord." But he said unto them, "Except I shall see in his hands the print of the nails, and put my finger into the print of the nails, and thrust my hand into his side, I will not believe"* (John 20:25).

When Jesus met with the disciples again, He instructed Thomas to touch Him.

> *Then saith he to Thomas, "Reach hither thy finger, and behold my hands; and reach hither thy hand, and thrust it into my side: and be not faithless, but believing." And Thomas answered and said unto him, "My Lord and my God." Jesus saith unto him, "Thomas, because thou hast seen me, thou hast believed: blessed are they that have not seen, and yet have believed"* (John 20:27–29).

Jesus was committed to Thomas even though Thomas had doubts about Him. Jesus did not avoid intimate contact with his doubting disciple. While Thomas was touching Jesus, Jesus was touching him, delivering the disciple from doubt and moving him to a new life of faith. Thomas became an apostle who preached the Gospel of Christ, the Risen Savior. Thomas just needed hands-on, one-on-one instruction on faith. Though he was in a doubtful state, Thomas had maintained connection with his fellow disciples. Thus, he was in the room when Jesus appeared again.

People struggling to overcome doubt can learn from Thomas the importance of staying connected to God and keeping fellowship with His believers. Stay involved in settings where believers magnify the Lord's presence and His instructions, including worship services, prayer circles, Bible studies, and outreach activities. Develop spiritual friendships with faith-filled people who know what it means to trust God no matter what. By doing these things, we are making ourselves available to receive doubt-destroying instructions from the Lord.

As He did with Thomas, the Lord uses touching moments to minister faith to us. He does not want us to avoid Him or to be condemned about our feelings. He wants us to touch Him deeply with our honesty, tears, and prayers for deliverance from doubt. He wants us to cling to His words and promises when we cannot see which way to go or understand how situations will work together for our good.

Sometimes we are like the man whose son was possessed and tormented by a demon since childhood. There seemed to be no hope for the boy. When Jesus' disciples could not deliver the son, the man's hope diminished. He was desperate, devastated, disappointed, and doubtful. Then came the Deliverer.

> *Jesus said unto him, "If thou canst believe, all things are possible to him that believeth." And straightway the father of the child cried out, and said with tears, "Lord, I believe; help thou mine unbelief"* (Mark 9:23–24).

Jesus delivered the man's son.

Nothing is impossible with the Lord. He can deliver us from doubt and instruct us on how to become strong in faith while facing life's challenges.

"I will not leave you comfortless; I will come to you" (John 14:18).

As the Lord comes to us, He calls us to Him. The Lord experienced humanity. Thus, He understands the challenges of being human. He has patience and compassion for us. We must trust that He truly can identify with us and will hear and help us.

> *Seeing then that we have a great high priest, that is passed into the heavens, Jesus the Son of God, let us hold fast our profession. For we have not an high priest which cannot be touched with the feeling of our infirmities; but was in all points tempted like as we are, yet without sin. Let us therefore come boldly unto the throne of grace, that we may obtain mercy, and find grace to help in time of need* (Heb. 4:14–16).

Let Us Pray

Thank You, Lord, for not abandoning us when we struggled with doubts. You have not forgotten the challenges of our humanity. You understand the depths of our emotions, needs, and sufferings. You choose to be touched with the feelings of our infirmities. Thank You, Lord, for coming to us with touching moments that reassure us, renew us in faith, and remind us that nothing is impossible with You.

Thank You for moving us from doubt to belief so that we can receive the wisdom You are releasing through Your Word and Your Holy Spirit.

Thank You for being so committed to our growth in You. You desire to show and teach us more. Yes, Lord, we want to receive more from You. Take us deeper in our touching relationship with you. Amen.

> *Thou hast dealt well with thy servant, O LORD, according unto thy word. Teach me good judgment and knowledge: for I have believed thy commandments* (Ps. 119:65-66).

More Touches, More Instructions

In the first lesson of this book, we saw how the Lord helped the apostle Peter escape prison and impending execution. While Peter was in prison, the saints unceasingly prayed for his life and release (Acts 12:5). The Lord answered by sending Peter an angel equipped with His touch and instructions.

The praying saints were "astonished" when Peter appeared at the door of the house where they were gathered (Acts 12:16). After Peter shared his deliverance experiences with them, he instructed them to tell the other apostles and church members of his deliverance. Then "he departed, and went into another place" (Acts 12:17). Through touch and instructions, Peter went from prison to freedom to another place.

As we obey instructions that come with the Lord's touches, our lives will go into another place He has prepared for us. He will free us to go to another place in faith, worship, and praise; another place in understanding, knowledge, and wisdom; another place in our relationships with others; and another place in surrendering ourselves to His love and obeying His will.

The Lord longs to bless us with more touches and more instructions. Like the potter who worked on the marred clay pottery, the Lord has us in His hands. He is touching us, instructing us, and making us into another vessel (Isa. 64:8; Jer. 18:1–6).

Our relationship with the Lord deepens as He enjoys our presence in His presence. He envelops us in His love. The Lord blesses us with His intimate touches of healing, peace, and comfort, while we glorify Him with worship, adoration, and devotion. The brightness of His glory shines on us as He leads us in His ways of righteousness and excellence.

Our obedience to the Lord will convey the testimony that we truly have been touched with instructions.

> *"I have taught thee in the way of wisdom; I have led thee in right paths ... Take fast hold of instruction; let her not go: keep her; for she is thy life"* (Prov. 4:11, 13).

Endnotes

Chapter 5

Zondervan's Compact Bible Dictionary (Grand Rapids, Mich.: Zondervan, 1993), p. 295, stating that the name Joseph means "may God add."

Zondervan's, p. 612. It is spelled "Zaphenath-Paneah" in *Zondervan's*, with reference to Genesis 41:45, meaning "the one who furnishes the sustenance of the land."

Zondervan's, p. 155, stating that Ephraim means "double fruit."

Chapter 15

Zondervan's, p. 304, stating that Kadesh means "be holy."

Chapter 20

Zondervan's, p. 435, where it is spelled Pasdammim, with reference to 1 Chronicles 11:13, meaning "place of bloodshed."

Zondervan's, p. 145, stating Eleazar means "God has helped."

Bibliography

Zondervan's Compact Bible Dictionary. Grand Rapids, Mich.: Zondervan, 1993.